RESTORE THE ESSENTIAL YOU

10

REASONS TO USE HYPNOTHERAPY

TO TRANSFORM YOUR LIFE

ANNE NYGREN DOHERTY

Author: Anne Nygren Doherty
Title: **Restore the Essential You:**
10 Reasons to Use Hypnotherapy to Transform Your Life
ISBN: 979-8-218-19319-5
Category: Self Care

Publisher:
Kindle Direct Publishing (KDP)

TABLE OF CONTENTS

DEDICATION

To John, Forever.

SIGNIFICANT STATEMENT

Often misunderstood, Hypnotherapy is an easy, effective means of improving the mind, body, and spirit. In this book, I show how and why it's so effective as well as 10 common applications for healing.

Acknowledgments

I would like to thank the founders of Hypnotherapy Academy of America, Tim and Angela Simmerman-Sierra, for providing such solid introductory professional training. Budding consciousness researcher, Danny Brosnahan, offered insightful comments for rewriting. My husband, John, lent his amazing eye to proofing and editing. My Sat Nam Rasayan teachers, Hargopal Khalsa and Patricia Dobrin, taught me what my hypnosis teachers later called "eastern hypnosis," but was really the most important thing I ever learned or experienced - that everything is connected, that human beings are all deeply and profoundly connected to each other, and that what we experience as our own life is really influenced by all of humanity. Thanks to my mom for starting me on this journey 50 years ago. Thanks to my dad for proving only just a few months ago that I'm right to still be on it.

PREFACE

I have been interested in hypnotherapy as a profession ever since I worked with a hypnotherapist in San Francisco many years ago. Working with her, I experienced a thrilling thought: "I can be a hypnotherapist myself!" Then, when I finally got around to studying hypnosis formally, I realized why I felt so drawn to this healing art—every important moment of my life somehow contributed to my understanding of hypnosis and executing it as a therapy on a high level.

As a young adult, I was exposed to talk therapy and psychiatry through my mother, who was falsely diagnosed with mental illness. I did talk therapy by myself on and off for years once I became an adult. Once married, my husband and I occasionally went for counseling together. When I acquired an autoimmune disease,

I quickly learned that western medical care does best when it's supported by alternative healing. I've experimented and found success with herbs, acupuncture, massage, and chiropractic. After the birth of my son, I struggled with hormone imbalance and ultimately became certified in Kundalini Yoga. We adopted our second child — a girl from China. Through her, I learned how birth trauma and the first months of life affect mindset and how sensory trauma affects the brain. My personal life had indeed trained me to be aware of how the mind affects the body.

I studied theater and music during college and writing in graduate school. I worked as a professional actor, and that whole experience exposed me to a wide variety of therapeutic techniques. In fact, I was exposed to what the rest of the world would consider novel thinking with respect to the body. To me, modalities like the Alexander Technique or the Feldenkrais Method were commonplace tools. But despite their effectiveness, the average person hasn't heard of them even today. And, so, to me, alternative healing modalities became equally important as the traditional.

The most important technique I've learned is still rare in the alternative healing community. It's called Sat Nam Rasayan, which, for lack of a better explanation, can be described as energy healing. Its name means Relaxation in the Name of Truth. In it, the practitioner goes into a meditative state and creates a relationship with the client. The relationship causes the practitioner to feel "resistances" - uncomfortable sensations, dreams, etc. - emotional and otherwise - in the body. Releasing this resistance causes healing in the client. Though my clients are usually unaware, I sometimes use this technique in my sessions to heighten results. What's important about Sat Nam Rasayan with respect to hypnosis is that it shows how human beings are energetically connected. Our thoughts, feelings, and physical state influence those things in the people around us and vice versa. Therefore, coming from a place of positive intent not only heals us, but it also improves life around us.

Now you can see how my entire life led to my becoming a hypnotherapist. Just doing the things I needed to do to grow up, be better in my career, and survive as a young woman raising a family exposed me to everything I needed to make a mark in this field. My life experience has shown me that most people are unaware of how much stress they carry, let alone how much their perceptions influence their behavior and the outcomes of their actions. Hypnosis is the easiest, fastest way to come into alignment. While it can provide amazing results, it's an easy first step to understanding the mysteries of the mind, body, and spirit connection.

WHAT ARE HYPNOSIS AND HYPNOTHERAPY?

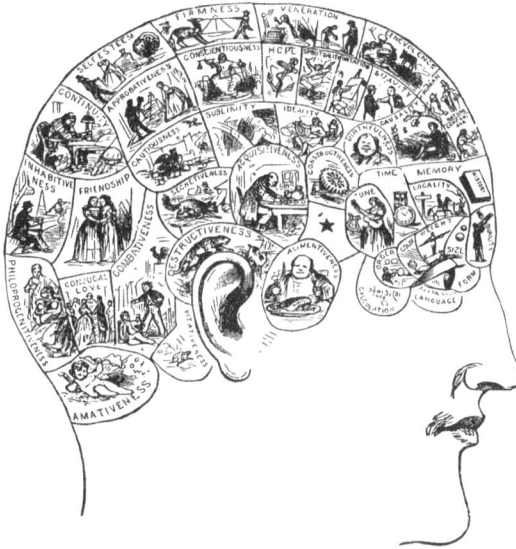

One of the more comical aspects of working as a hypnotherapist is discovering what neighbors, friends, and potential clients believe - and fear - about hypnosis. Even some scientists and medical professionals suddenly let go of their education and experiential knowledge of how the brain works and confess they are afraid that, in a hypnotic trance, they will float away, never wake up, or turn into some kind of zombie. They recall bar mitzvahs or college events in which a hypnotist made some portion of the audience do ridiculous things. For example, the first time I saw a stage hypnotist, he got my friend to "bark like a chicken." These professionals simultaneously think hypnosis is ridiculous and that the hypnotist has magical powers. In fact, someone I deeply respect told me he thought hypnosis was black magic and couldn't understand how someone as smart as I am could be drawn to the dark side.

Comically, their fears just prove how the subconscious mind works. In a vulnerable moment, something makes an impression, and otherwise rational people let go of all reason. Know this: the most important things to remember about hypnosis are 1) it's natural, and 2) no one can get you to do anything you don't want to do. One must agree with subconscious programming for it to occur. Yes, even when asked to bark like a chicken.

So, what is hypnosis, and how does it work? What exactly is hypnotherapy?

Hypnosis is a time-tested method - used by doctors and psychiatric professionals since German physician Franz Mesmer developed it to heal patients in the late 18th century. Doctors used hypnosis to work with victims of shell shock during WWI, WWII, and the Korean War. Important pioneers in the fields of movement, like Moishe Feldenkrais, and psychology, like Milton Erickson, considered hypnosis the keystone of their work.

By definition, hypnosis is "a Natural State of Mind in which deep relaxation diminishes the Critical Factor so that the mind can focus on Suggestions." Let's unpack that definition bit by bit.

What do I mean by "Natural State of Mind"? Trance is measurable by any device that reads brain waves, such as an electroencephalography (EEG) device. These devices make an electrogram of the spontaneous electrical activity of the brain; in other words, they read your brain activity, measured in waves, and can tell whether you are awake (beta waves) or asleep (delta waves), in a trance (alpha and theta waves), functioning in a peak state (gamma waves).[1] If you were to wear an EEG device throughout the day, you would discover that you naturally go into trance multiple times a day. Just before you wake up and just before you fall asleep are two examples of trance; it makes sense that to get from beta to delta, one would have to go through alpha and theta. But other examples of alpha waves include: 1) anytime you look at a screen device, 2) when you get deeply involved in a sporting or theatrical event, and 3) when you drive a car home and, thinking about something the entire way, you aren't exactly sure how you got home.

HUMAN BRAIN WAVES

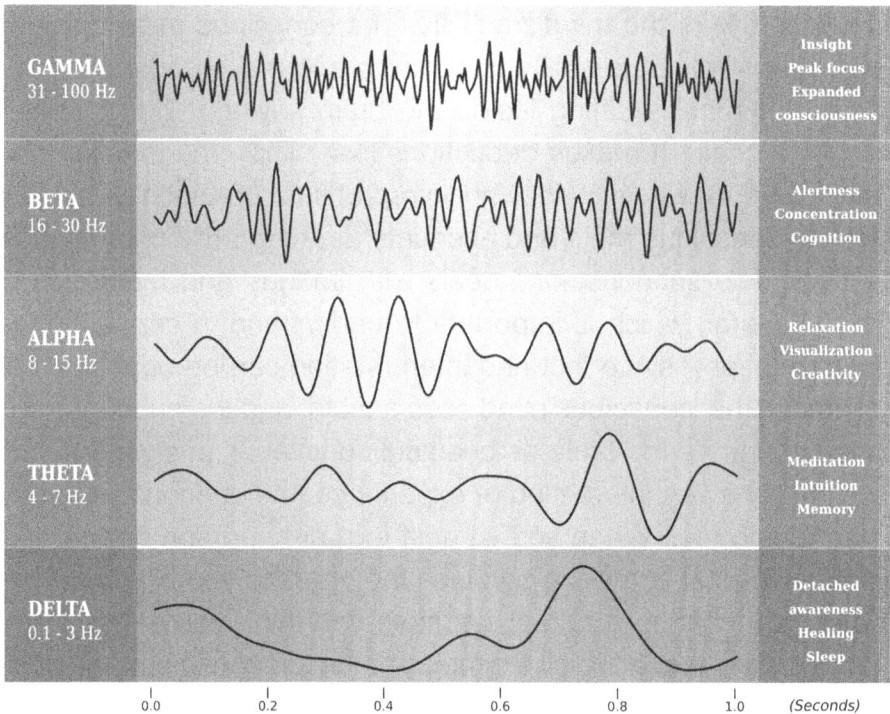

GAMMA 31 - 100 Hz		Insight Peak focus Expanded consciousness
BETA 16 - 30 Hz		Alertness Concentration Cognition
ALPHA 8 - 15 Hz		Relaxation Visualization Creativity
THETA 4 - 7 Hz		Meditation Intuition Memory
DELTA 0.1 - 3 Hz		Detached awareness Healing Sleep

0.0   0.2   0.4   0.6   0.8   1.0   (Seconds)

[1] https://www.scientificamerican.com/article/what-is-the-function-of-t-1997-12-22/

Relaxation matters because it facilitates focus. But as we see from the above examples, the body doesn't have to be completely relaxed for the brain to go into trance. When we are relaxed, we soften what is known as the Critical Factor or the Analytical Mind.

The Critical Factor is basically the rules and beliefs gathered up over a lifespan. When you experience an event, the Critical Factor compares and contrasts that experience to previous ones in order for the mind to know how to react or feel.

The "mind" is a simple word used to describe the brain's cognitive functions. If the mind is in charge of our cognitive abilities, think of the mind as having two parts: the conscious and the subconscious. The conscious mind is surprisingly small, taking up 5 to 10% of the mind's activity. The conscious mind includes our free will plus the ability to perceive and make deductions. It's as if someone is sitting inside the brain saying, "That's a tree. That's a chair." It makes deductions like, "That tree is taller than my house." However, it does not interpret. Interpretation belongs to the subconscious mind and accounts for 90 to 95% of the mind's activity. The subconscious deals with images and memories. It is very literal, which is important to understand in connection to interpretation - since fact and interpretation can be opposite. For example, the conscious mind sees a table, and the subconscious mind interprets the table as beautiful, functional, in style, etc. So, in virtually every interaction or experience, the subconscious tells you how to feel. When you sit next to a dirty person on the bus, when you trust someone because they remind you of Aunt Alice, when you choose a career because you think you're good at a certain skill - these are all examples of the subconscious in action.

The subconscious deals with memories. Therefore, it's a

storehouse of all that is good, bad, or indifferent in our lives. When we have an experience, the conscious mind sends sensory information to the Critical Factor, which compares and contrasts the event to previous experiences. If the event makes an impact, the subconscious records it for future comparison. If the event is similar to previous events, the subconscious labels it as being in the same category as those earlier events. If we can't recognize the event at all, the subconscious mind rejects it. So, it is easy to see how misunderstandings and misinterpretations occur. For example, if an ax murderer has blue eyes and a twinkling smile like Uncle Joe, you might not notice he's got an ax in his hand. In another vein, if you're offered a lucrative job in which a small part requires public speaking and your 6th grade teacher pilloried your speech about Presidents' Day, you might prefer to live in poverty than ever stand in front of a crowd again.

A hypnotherapist helps a client identify negative beliefs that may be contributing to some kind of self-sabotage - over-eating, for example, or picking fights with your spouse. The therapist and the client together determine what the client wants instead - the reversal of the negative behavior - and together, they craft suggestions for positive beliefs and behavior. The therapist takes the client into trance and delivers the suggestions. In another type of session, the therapist guides the client to recall a negative experience from the past and re-experience it in a positive light. In fact, there are dozens of session types - but each one has the same goal of transforming the negative into the positive. Hypnosis works because, as the Indian yogi Sadhguru says, "Self-transformation is not just about changing yourself. It means shifting to a completely new dimension of experience and perception." This means that changing behavior or appearances alone is not enough. A true, deep transformation is necessary to achieve goals. Hypnosis provides that vehicle for deep transformation.

Let's take a look at two very recent studies:

First, in 2018, an NIH-backed study that the Hypnotherapy Academy of America did with the University of New Mexico on bladder control reveals that short-term (two months) hypnosis performed equally to medicine, that patients who did both medicine and hypnotherapy improved at a much higher rate than either alone, but that over the long term (12 months), hypnotherapy actually fared better than medicine alone. [2]

Second, also in 2018, weight loss research done by Irving Kirsch, director of the Program in Placebo Studies at Harvard Medical School, compared hypnotherapy to cognitive behavior therapy (CBT). It found that combining hypnosis and CBT led to the greatest weight loss. However, those who did hypnotherapy, whether with or without CBT, maintained the weight loss for the 18-month follow-up. Those with CBT alone gained weight back. [3]

The deep relaxation experienced in hypnosis weakens the Critical Factor, and therefore, false, limiting, or unwanted beliefs held in the subconscious can be altered or even dropped, freeing the client to relate to the world in completely new and desired ways. In the case of weight loss, for example, a client may falsely believe he is trapped in a body that can never lose weight, or another may believe a layer of fat protects her from sexual assault. By working with a hypnotherapist to uncover and reshape your individual subconscious belief system, you may suddenly find exercise and diet easier to follow, as well as more effective.

---

[2] https://www.ncbi.nlm.nih.gov/pmc/articles/PMC4575591/
[3] https://time.com/5380312/is-hypnosis-real-science/

HOW PROGRAMMING - OR ACCEPTED BELIEFS - APPEAR IN THE BRAIN

But how does negative programming occur?

Negative programming occurs in 6 ways:

1. The Authority Figure. It might be a teacher, your parents, older relatives, a religious figure, a politician, a boss, or anyone with power you admire. Their words and deeds make an impact.

2. The Peer Group. You remember peer pressure from middle school and high school. But you still experience it - if you identify with a religion or political party, or work for a large corporation or have a close-knit neighborhood or set of friends.

3. Situations of High Emotion. Both trauma and blessings make an impact on the subconscious, helping us stay safe in the future.

4. Repetition. If we hear a statement often enough, we begin to believe it, even if it's a lie.

5. Saying Yes to an Idea. For all of the above, some part of us has to agree with the programming. For example, if a teacher calls a child stupid, and the child agrees, "Yes, I

am," then "I'm stupid" becomes part of the programming. So, while we may be innocent when these events occur, we must agree for the impression to stick.

6. The Hypnotic State. With the Critical Factor relaxed, new programming occurs more easily.

Let's look at an example of how programming occurs.

Imagine that in second grade you get a "C" on your first spelling test. Your parents yell at you - maybe your teacher, too. That's the authority figures. If your friends make fun of you, that's peer pressure. Their behavior creates a highly emotional situation that makes you feel bad about yourself and so awful about spelling you can't bring yourself to study for the next test. So, you get another "C." Now repetition becomes part of the programming, and before you know it, a vicious cycle begins. You begin to agree with others that you're no good at spelling, and that means you've said "yes" to a false belief. Now that idea is planted firmly in your subconscious, and it will take the planting of another belief to reverse it.

Now you can see that once programming happens, the mind becomes like a computer that makes predictions - whether you predict that you'll always get "C's" in spelling or that you don't deserve a raise you desperately need, or that living with a crippling disease is just your fate. British Neuroscientist Anil Seth calls consciousness "controlled hallucination." The sharing of experiences (I see a table/you see a table) means consciousness has limitations and controls. But whether the table is ugly, pretty, the right shade, or has a special meaning is all a kind of hallucination unique to each individual.

Now, imagine hundreds of thousands - if not millions - of people experiencing those same six influences, and it's easy to see how mass hypnosis can occur. Some people simply lack the time, and others lack the ability, to research everything that comes into their awareness. We simply have to make judgments to get along in the world. However, carrying the knowledge of how programming works can help individuals remain less attached to opinions and perceptions so they can protect themselves from mass influences like social media and video technologies.

In addition to the conscious and subconscious minds, there is also the "superconscious," which we can think of as nestled within the subconscious. The superconscious feels like a state of flow. It is your true self. While your subconscious may take in negative programming, your core self always remains the same, which is why negative programming can trigger anxiety, depression, or illness. Basically, negative programming from trauma or childhood events prevents access to the superconscious. Hypnosis takes down the wall of negativity to restore a sense of flow.

The takeaway here is that you are you and that, even in hypnosis, you always remain who you are. Working with a hypnotherapist, the client is like a co-therapist. With guidance, the client sets the agenda and has complete control because no one can be hypnotized to do or believe anything against their will. If a hypnotherapist attempts to do so, the client most likely will snap out of trance. If the client stays in trance, it's likely that the client agrees on some level with the programming or has some other reason for not immediately addressing the situation - perhaps an unwillingness to confront the therapist. In any case, the client remarks inwardly that the suggestion doesn't apply, and only if the client agrees with the suggestion will it have an impact.

As Milton Erickson said, "Patients are patients because they are out of rapport with their own subconscious…they are people who have had too much programming - so much outside programming they have lost touch with their inner selves."

Let's walk through another example, starting with an undesired situation or result. Let's imagine I have an eating disorder. I'm terribly underweight but think I'm fat. I'm too thin because I hardly eat and I drink only water. I do this because of the powerful emotions I feel around my appearance. I'm afraid of rejection. I'm afraid of being humiliated. I'm afraid of life being out of control. I'm terrified. Why? Because deep down I believe I'm no good and unlovable. When I was little, I was chubby. And my family and friends made fun of me. I was told I was ugly and no one would ever want to love me. So, you can see how my eating disorder may be my responsibility, but it isn't exactly my fault. When I was tiny and didn't know better, I trusted the people around me and believed the negative things they said about me.

Now, if we can use hypnotherapy as a new event, we can create a new belief - that I'm lovable and fine the way I am - which leads to a new emotion of peace and contentment, that leads to new desired behaviors - such as my eating delicious foods that strengthen and fuel my body. As a result, my body becomes healthy, and I have a sound, accurate body image. Additionally, I project that I love myself, I attract people who appreciate me, and my entire life changes for the better.

With hypnosis, we can change negative programming to positive and create the life we want.

Now that you know what hypnosis is, you know what it is not. It is not stage theatrics, and it's not black magic. It's not going to lead to the zombie apocalypse. Instead, it's a scientifically proven meditative method in which you are the co-therapist who changes your own life for the better.

THE REASONS

1

It's Good, Fast and Cheap

"Most people spend more time and energy going around problems than in trying to solve them."

— HENRY FORD

Good, fast, and cheap - or the "Iron Triangle" as it's called in MBA programs - is hard to find in any item or service. When I was in graduate school studying theater production, one of my teachers said, "If something is good, fast, and cheap, grab it." Usually, buyers get only one or two of those: if something is good and cheap, you don't tend to get it very quickly; if something is good and fast, it's going to be expensive; if something is fast and cheap, it's not likely to be very good. And what if a buyer only gets one? Which one should they choose? Dozens of business websites advise buyers what to choose - good, fast, or cheap - and why!

When I first experienced hypnosis, my therapist promised results in as little as 3 sessions. I experienced very good results for my goal at the time - good enough to inspire me to look into hypnosis as a career. But this woman was not trained in medical support, as I am, and the truth was I needed several more sessions to make an impact on my health. If I was assessing a case like mine today, I'd recommend 10. Ultimately, I found someone who did recommend 10, and I had amazing results, despite the fact I was under enormous stress at the time.

Just before I started the 10 sessions, I had been seeing a talk therapist, whom I thought to be one of the best in my experience. But still, something was lacking. I knew how I wanted my behavior to change, and yet I wasn't transforming. Results were slow, and the therapist was guessing I'd need to see him for two more years. That time frame seemed daunting to me - financially as well as with respect to my goals and self-esteem. But hypnotherapy also seemed daunting; each session would be 2 hours long, so they cost twice as much as the talk therapy. But I took a risk and was glad I did. In about 3 months, my behavior had changed. I was satisfied and no longer needed assistance.

Now, look at the finances and the time. A single hypnosis session cost me twice what one session with my talk therapist cost at that time. However, my hypnotherapy sessions were twice as long time-wise, plus I received personalized recordings and other advice. So, each session, in my opinion, did 5 times the heavy lifting because I could work on my issue as much as I was able - one, two or even three times a day. I went to sessions weekly or bi-weekly over several months instead of weekly sessions for several years. My life didn't become perfect or problem free; that would've been an unreasonable goal as no life is ever free from problems. However, with hypnotherapy, my ability to handle what life dished out felt like it went up 1000%. I recognize that in terms of science, my experience is n=1, meaning I'm the only person in a study in which I'm also in charge of the experiment. But my experience impressed me enough to study hypnosis and make it my life's work.

Handling life well should be the real point of any therapy. I believe a therapist's goal should be to get patients to function in the shortest time possible, yet most talk therapists see themselves as more or less a permanent fixture in their patients' lives. Less ethical talk therapists may even create codependent relationships that lead clients to think they need the therapist to function. Sometimes a patient can take months to discover whether or not a talk therapist is a good match. While I believe that talk therapy is great for anyone who needs to develop self-awareness and essential for people in crisis, I have experienced the frustration of trying to find that special therapeutic someone. In my n=1 experience, I've found it takes a therapist about three months – or 12 weeks – to even begin to know me or fully understand my problem.

In the hands of a good hypnotherapist, however, clients will discover that hypnotherapy is one of those rare services: it's good, fast, and cheap. It's good because it works. It's fast because hypnotherapists help clients achieve goals in a limited time frame - often in 3 to 10 sessions. And since it takes less time than traditional talk therapy, it saves a lot of money and is therefore cheap, even if the per session out-of-pocket may be comparable or higher.

A good hypnotherapist will quickly steer clients needing talk therapy to appropriate treatment. Hypnotherapy is particularly ideal for people who have a clear goal and know that they are standing in the way of that goal. It's less suitable for people who need or have become dependent on psychotropic drugs, don't know what's wrong with themselves, or are completely unwilling to accept that their emotions and mind-set affect the outcome of their actions. Many people do accept this, however. So, why should they spend years in talk therapy? Why not go straight to the heart of what is standing in a client's way? And why not take 3 to 10 sessions to do this, compared to weekly sessions with a talk therapist for over a period of 1 to 2 years?

In my practice, sessions last two hours, and my hourly rate matches that of the less expensive therapists in my town. The high-end talk therapists charge double my 2-hour session rate for just one hour. That means if clients receive my maximum 10 sessions per goal, they pay the equivalent of 20 weeks of services from less expensive therapists. Compare that two 52 weeks - or even 104 weeks - of talk therapy.

With both hypnosis and talk therapy, clients usually come away with a deeper understanding of their problem, but understanding it is not the point – fixing it is. Trying to understand a problem in depth is a waste of time for most issues. You already know what you know about it. For instance, if you were abused as a child, you already know it was a bad experience. All the programming resulting from the trauma and abuse causes your behavior to go awry. Hypnosis can go back and neutralize or even reverse your emotional relationship to those key events and people, giving you strong boundaries and positive inner resources.

When I was a young wife, my husband and I saw a talk therapist we thought was excellent. He promoted strong character and had little tolerance for excuses. He said people don't suffer so much from lost memories (a hot topic during that day) - it's what they remember that haunts them. He recommended that when we see a problem, we should acknowledge it and step around it. I agree with him on those points. The trouble is that most people don't know how to step around their problem. It's the little behaviors and perceptions that perpetuate the problem. For example, let's say I'm in an abusive relationship. My partner says cruel things to me, and that makes me cry. However, I may not realize that I choose to stay in this relationship because I have some kind of attraction or connection to the abuser.

On the other hand, I may not realize that my tone of voice is what causes my partner to yell. I'm so afraid of my partner that I project fear, and that makes my partner feel unloved or disrespected. Perhaps my fear of close relationships started when I was very small, and I don't even remember how or why it all began. Each client's reasons for doing what they do is absolutely unique.

So, if I use hypnosis to change my relationship with the abuser on a fundamental, subconscious level, I automatically engage in new behaviors. I may decide to leave the relationship. Or my voice changes and the partner no longer feels threatened, and the relationship changes for the better. Just as each client's reasons for arriving in a poor relationship are unique, so are their solutions to the problem. There's no time spent on moral judgment or what society finds acceptable; solutions discovered in hypnosis are the client's own solutions. A client could talk for years and years, and all that might happen is that the idea of being stuck in an abusive relationship gets reinforced by all the talk. In hypnotherapy, clients heal themselves.

I'm not saying that talk therapy doesn't work or that it wastes time. I'm saying that people who already have some awareness about their situation or their inability to achieve their goals might be able to solve their problems more quickly and easily, and with less trauma, via hypnotherapy.

Of course, like other psychological healing modalities, both hypnosis and talk therapy depend most on the rapport between therapist and client - even above a therapist's training or skill. No matter the cost or time involved, it's better for clients to solve their problems with the therapist they have faith in. Hypnotherapists, like talk therapists, are human, and some of them may be badly trained, inexperienced or ignorant. But if I had to choose between a flawed talk therapist and a flawed hypnotherapist, I would choose the hypnotherapist because at least I'd discover quickly whether this person will be of help.

Another advantage of hypnotherapy is that there is little danger of creating a codependent relationship with your therapist. The whole idea of hypnotherapy is success in as few sessions as possible. I want my clients to be independent and spread the word about how great it feels to be free in body, mind, and spirit. I want them to refer their friends, family, and coworkers so that I have a comfortable stream of clients rotating in and out of my practice. I don't want them to feel they have to come back to me again and again and again and again because they can't stand on their own.

Though I hope my clients do return to me when they have new, hard-to-reach goals, I don't want them as permanent fixtures in my office or to depend on them for my income.

Another great advantage of hypnosis over talk therapy, which I'll explore later, is that clients really heal themselves. The hypnotherapist is simply a guide or a tool for that self-healing. This means that it doesn't really matter what my hypnotherapist thinks about a wide range of topics or personal situations. Hypnotherapists who are true to their job should be neutral about the client's life situation or abstain from handling clients that upset them. If my talk therapist is an atheist and I am a Christian or the other way around, at some point, we might come to blows. I may go months before I realize that my therapist, who had dutifully presented a neutral front in the beginning, in fact disrespects a part of my life I value deeply. As a result, I might feel betrayed, frustrated, or abandoned. With hypnotherapy, the idea is to quickly and effectively facilitate the client's healing or behavior change. While I've been trained not to give advice, the truth is there isn't much time to do it, even if I suddenly want to. The act of honing the client's goals and delivering the sessions, plus the pressure of time, requires me to stay neutral.

The belief that each life is valuable and on earth for a purpose is a cornerstone of my approach. My job is to connect you to your higher self and that purpose. It's there…and we just have to discover and set it free by putting it into words. Where opinion or interpretation comes into my work is deciding how best to get the client from A (the problem) to B (the goal); that is, down which path should I guide the client to reverse the false beliefs and negative subconscious programming that contributes to the client's lack of connection to purpose and natural gifts.

That's like deciding which road to take to get to a certain destination. That the destination exists is self-evident, and no judgment is attached to it. You jump into my therapeutic taxi, as it were, and I decide the best, fastest way to take you there so that when you arrive, you're happy to be there and make the most of your experience.

A client came to me with IBS symptoms that he'd been experiencing for 20 years - the three most recent years on a daily basis. He had been to every appropriate kind of doctor and had had every kind of test. Everyone told him his digestive system was perfect - he had perfect flora, the walls of his colon were blemish free, etc. I told him I thought he'd need 8 to 10 sessions to experience relief. At 6, we knew we were close to ending. At 7, we parted ways. He went from experiencing intestinal agony several times a day to perhaps experiencing a mild problem every two weeks.

Once the symptoms began to subside, it soon became clear to him what emotional situations caused them. He even began to take care of his body differently - during one session, a protocol I created for the vagus nerve, he suddenly blurted out, "I need to drink more water!" After the session, he revealed he had only been drinking wine and coffee. He wondered why no doctor had ever asked him about his drinking habits. Whether they never did, or because of psychological blocks he never heard the question, doesn't matter. What matters is that his subconscious mind told him to drink eight glasses of water a day and give himself permission to enjoy retirement, which resulted in more healthy digestion.

What made this man's experience so successful was his full participation in the program. He practiced self-hypnosis twice a day and every time he had symptoms. He understood that hypnosis is a tool anyone can master and that, if he learned its ropes, he could use it for other goals after his IBS was healed. In short, hypnosis was a tool he could use throughout his life. So, regarding the iron triangle of Good, Fast, and Cheap, he not only completed his goal in fewer sessions than anticipated, he embraced a tool that would save him pain, time, and money in the future.

So, when choosing any form of therapy, it's a good idea to ask what the end game looks like. Ask yourself these questions before talking to any therapist: 1) What results do I want or are reasonable to expect? 2) How much do I expect to spend? 3) How much time do I expect the process to take? Then, begin your hunt with an open mind, and when you think you've found the right person, do that math. Do this therapist's recommendations match your expectations? Why or why not?

Finding the right person matters most. If you don't have a good rapport to the extent that you can be completely honest with your therapist, you won't engage, and whatever money you spend is wasted. I give a free 20-minute consultation to make sure that the client and I are well-matched, that the client's goals are realistic, and that the client leaves with a good guess about the cost and number of sessions.

I encourage good communication about time and money throughout so that my client is comfortable with the entire process. In fact, I have a saying from my theater days, when I used to rent a venue to artists: "If you can't talk about money, you just can't talk." If a therapist doesn't appear to respect your financial situation, either you have unrealistic goals, you could be headed for disappointment, or both. A good hypnotherapist will work with you so that you know what to expect, so your experience truly is good, fast, and cheap.

2

It's Relaxing

*"Learn to relax. Your body is precious,
as it houses your mind and spirit. Inner peace
begins with a relaxed body."*

—NORMAN VINCENT PEALE

When I was a little girl, stores were closed on Sundays, and of course, there was no Internet. Really, there was nothing to do except go to church, read the Sunday paper, and have a nice lunch with the family. I remember summer Sundays in which we, as a family, just sat on the porch, lightly snoozing and gently talking. Even my workaholic father took relaxation fairly seriously; on Sunday, he didn't do briefs or make calls.

Today, however, in the western world, we no longer encourage relaxation as part of a healthy life. In the 1970s, after more women began to work, stores began opening on Sundays; and certainly, after the invention of the Internet, Sunday activities changed from prayer and relaxation to families catching up with all that couldn't be done during the week. And, of course, the Internet encourages us to keep searching, keep shopping, and keep clicking, sometimes long after our interest has waned. People under 40 today hardly remember a time without cell phones; indeed, for many, the cell phone has become almost like an appendage.

When I first saw a hypnotherapist, I was surprised – actually, shocked – to realize how tense I really was. After all, I do yoga every day, and I meditate. Yet, when guided into trance, I felt emotional reactions from the act of relaxation itself. When I relaxed, I could feel my truth, as it were. I could be fully honest with myself. I recognized that, if necessary, I should schedule relaxation until it became a natural part of my daily routine. I relax for 10 minutes after yoga. I relax whenever I eat a meal (I do not eat and work.) And I relax before bed - which gives me a good night's sleep.

Once I became a hypnotherapist, I quickly saw that I was not alone in that reaction – that most people really don't know how to relax. And, without relaxation, we are destined for trouble.

Relaxation reduces stress and the symptoms of mental health conditions like depression, anxiety, and schizophrenia. Relaxation also has other related health benefits, including: [4]

- lowering heart rate, blood pressure and breathing rate
- reducing muscle tension and chronic pain
- improving concentration and mood
- reducing fatigue
- reducing anger and frustration
- boosting confidence to handle problems

A 1986 New York Times article showcasing the results of multiple studies made me wonder why all these years later doctors aren't more focused on anything that can induce relaxation. [5] One study showed that, in asthmatics, for example, relaxation training was found to widen restricted respiratory passages. In some people with diabetes, relaxation can reduce the need for insulin. In many patients with chronic, unbearable pain, relaxation brings about significant relief. Relaxation may help ward off disease by making people less susceptible to viruses and lowering blood pressure and cholesterol levels.

The sympathetic nervous system takes care of the body under stress. It reacts to stress by secreting hormones that mobilize the body's muscles and organs to face a threat. Sometimes called the "fight-or-flight response," this mobilization includes a variety of biological responses, including shifting blood flow from the limbs to the organs and increased blood pressure. The stress response does not require an emergency; it can be triggered merely by everyday worries and pressures.

---

[4] healthdirect.gov.au,
[5] https://www.nytimes.com/1986/05/13/science/relaxation-surprising-benefits-detected.html

Relaxation stimulates the parasympathetic nervous system - which helps us feed, breed, rest, and digest. A relaxation response releases muscle tension, lowers blood pressure and slows the heart and breath rates. It shifts hormone levels that seem to produce beneficial effects on the immune system. For example, according to a report in the Journal of Behavioral Medicine,[6] relaxation training in medical students during exams was found to increase their levels of helper cells that defend against infectious diseases. The degree of benefits depends on the depth to which people use the relaxation techniques. Those medical students who used the techniques just a few times showed little or no changes in their immune measure. Those who did the exercises faithfully had the strongest immune effects.

In another study, Ohio State researchers taught relaxation techniques to retirement home residents, whose average age was 74 years. After a month of training, their levels of natural killer cells and antibody titers - indicators of resistance to tumors and viruses - had improved significantly, according to a report in Health Psychology Journal.[7]

Much interest in the medical use of relaxation has been for patients suffering from cardiovascular problems. A report in the British Medical Journal, for example, reported that patients who had been trained to relax significantly lowered their blood pressure and had maintained that reduction four years later.[8]

---

[6] https://link.springer.com/article/10.1023/A:1018700829825
[7] https://www.nytimes.com/1986/05/13/science/relaxation-surprising-benefits-detected.html
[8] https://www.bmj.com/content/300/6736/1368

Research at the Harvard Medical School[9] found that regular sessions of a simple meditation technique decreased the body's response to norepinephrine, a hormone released in reaction to stress. Although the endocrine system continued to emit the hormones, they did not have their usual effects.

Of course, one of the major boons of relaxation training - and one of the most sought-after results from hypnotherapy - is lessening or alleviating chronic, severe pain. Such pain can arise from many different causes, including backache, chronic migraine or tension headaches, diseases such as cancer, and even the unintended outcome of operations. Yet, nearly all types of pain respond to some degree to relaxation. Why? Because pain begets pain. In the later chapter on pain, I explain why this is so. But let's apply that theory to stress and say, "stress begets stress." The more stress you perceive the more stress you experience. It's a vicious circle that the experience of relaxation could break.

How does hypnotherapy improve the client's ability to relax? Hypnosis requires relaxation in order to be effective. A session typically starts with some form of relaxation - called an Induction - which induces a trance state in the client. That's followed by more relaxation, often in the form of images, called "deepening." Only when clients are fully relaxed can the parasympathetic nervous system kick in and the Critical Factor relax so that the hypnotherapist can guide the clients to retrain the subconscious.

In the healing states of alpha and theta brain waves, clients experience the super-conscious, true self, or state of flow.

---

[9] https://sitn.hms.harvard.edu/flash/2009/issue61/

Hypnosis can also help the client relax on a regular basis outside of the hypnotherapist's office by reversing whatever keeps the client from relaxing in the first place. I'd say about half of my clients experience some form of poor sleep. Setting aside any physical reasons, like obstructive sleep apnea, the rest don't sleep well thanks to some form of stress. If we change the relationship to that stress, the sleep problem often resolves on its own indirectly.

One aging client had heart issues, bladder issues, and high blood pressure. In addition to her own health, she also took care of her husband who was going blind. She was a devout Catholic. In her first session, we created a suggestion utilizing the Holy Spirit. The moment that she allied herself with the Holy Spirit, her perception of all of her issues improved and, within just 3 sessions, she achieved all of her highly reasonable goals: her blood pressure returned to normal, she woke only once a night (as opposed to 3 or 4 times), and her heart doctor gave her permission to travel.

Since her goals were reasonable and she didn't wish she was 30 years younger, for example. it was easy for her to accept them in light of her belief system and her affirmations. The stress stopped along with her perception of it.

Talk therapy would be of little or no use to this client. She knew what her problem was: she was an old woman taking care of an old man whom she loved dearly. She simply wanted all that to go as smoothly as possible. Her worry made her perception of stress worse, and it was likely that talk therapy would only heighten the worry simply because she might be asked to talk about her problems over and over. As I said, she knew what her problem was; so why explain it more than once? And, the solution was simple: connect her to a resource within her belief system. The second she put herself in God's hands, her perception of stress diminished.

One might ask if an atheist can receive the same results. The answer is "yes," provided we tap into a resource within that client's belief system. In place of God, some clients draw on "the universe" or "energy," but I've also helped clients connect with "forgiveness" or "the Tao." We might even have to go back to the client's childhood to tap into such a resource, but that resource certainly exists because hypnosis shares the same brain frequencies as meditation and prayer. It's measurable, and although a small portion of people resist hypnosis, everyone experiences trance states multiple times a day.[10]

Another client, who happened to be bipolar, came to me with the goal of decreasing her medications. She had full permission from her psychiatrist to do this; the doctor and I were in communication, and I referred her to acupuncture for physical support. Unfortunately, during this time, so much stress rained down upon this client - friends and family dying and/or contracting life-threatening illnesses, changes in her living situation, changes in finances, and more - that her original goal became unrealistic. We agreed it would not be wise to try to reduce psychiatric medication while she had so much stress in her life. Her short-term goal changed to finding resources that would help her deal with stress and learn to relax. Individuals with bipolar often have trouble relaxing because their minds may hop from topic to topic. This client specifically spoke of being unable to sit still and meditate, as many of her friends belonged to a meditation group.

---

[10] https://anxietycontrolcenter.com/can-anyone-go-into-a-trance-6/

Initially, this woman took her hypnosis practice very seriously, doing self-hypnosis several times a day. To calm her digestion, which was already upset due to the medication, she learned to go into trance on her own, without the use of recordings. In our sessions, we went back to her childhood and discovered inner resources, and she began to see that her perception of her stress was almost as bad as the stress itself. Soon, she was handling her life with grace and ease, getting a decent night's sleep, experiencing improved digestion, and meditating for 10 minutes or so every day.

So, if the only benefit a client gains from hypnosis is learning to relax, that's a good enough reason to do it. Regard the trance induction process as a kind of lesson in relaxation and you will quickly learn to relax yourself even under trying situations. If there's a reason relaxation is difficult for you, hypnosis can help you discover and reverse it. Then, relaxation as a tool will be more readily accessible to you. Soon you will sleep more deeply and restoratively. You will be more present in conversations with friends or at work. You will breathe better, and your health will improve. It's worth it.

③

It Reduces Stress

*"If you are distressed by anything external,
the pain is not due to the thing itself but to your own
estimate of it; and this you have the power
to revoke at any moment."*

—MARCUS AURELIUS

My dictionary defines stress as "a state of mental or emotional strain or tension resulting from adverse or demanding circumstances." Yet, whether something is demanding is a matter of perception. Perception depends on how the body and mind experience events. By mind, I mean the subconscious.

If you enjoy history, as I do, you may often ask yourself how people from another time endured. Let's say you lived as a farm wife in the great plains of the United States in the 1870s. You would have certain expectations, and because you did, your life was easier than we might think from our 21st-century vantage point. You would expect to milk cows, churn butter, make your own clothes, wash them by hand, and boil diapers, while your husband worked the fields, managed the money, and voted.

Life was hard; but you expected it to be. Physical endurance might've been something you'd seen or known all your life. So, while you may not live to a ripe old age, you wouldn't expect to. You may be exhausted; but you're not necessarily "stressed." You'd be stressed if you became ill and got behind in your work. You'd be stressed if the weather obliterated the crops your husband worked so hard to raise. In short, you'd be stressed by falling short of your own expectations.

It's good to have expectations. In fact, we need them to get through our day. Because I expect a red traffic light to turn green, I wait patiently. If the light doesn't turn green after a reasonable time, I think the light is broken and venture carefully into the intersection.

Expectations when they're unreasonable - when they deny the reality in front of you - can go very wrong. Let's say it's 1880. You're the daughter of a wealthy mill owner in Connecticut. You have what amounts to a high school education, and at some event in your town, you meet a wealthy rancher from Texas who is visiting his family after the death of a beloved relative. In those days, the man would stay months on a visit because travel was so challenging. You fall in love, marry against your father's wishes, and the man takes you back to Texas.

There, you come up against every expectation your subconscious ever formed, as well as patterns learned by your body. It takes days for you both to travel there. Once you arrive, the weather feels all wrong. The landscape is unfamiliar. And, although your husband doesn't expect you to milk cows, you have to manage a household where everything seems foreign to you - all the while engaging with a community with unfamiliar social expectations. Some people speak Spanish. Some natives speak only their own tongue. You don't know how to communicate. Though your life is physically easier than that of the farm wife in the great plains, you're under extreme stress because your subconscious mind keeps projecting the wrong expectations. You're a fish out of water.

Stress is also a matter of how one's body experiences events. For example, I have a mild heart murmur. I was diagnosed with it at age 17. However, no one told me what that meant in terms of my perception until I was about 40. The heart doctor told me that sudden shocks would affect me more than they would other people, and that sometimes I might experience emotions I didn't believe in. By this point in my life, I was already deeply into psychology, yoga, and meditation. When I heard these words, it became apparent why I had been drawn to studying the mind: I had always suspected that my perception of stress was different from that of others.

In school, the other kids would make fun of me if I burst out crying after being hit in the head with a ball. Even I didn't believe in being shocked by such an inconsequential event. Yet, I found that if I didn't sit down and calm my emotions, I would be a mess the rest of the day. Today, if I experience a sudden shock, I expect to have a reaction others might call extreme. However, after all of these years of adjusting my expectations about sudden shocks, I rarely have what I would call an extreme reaction. I just do what my body requires to deal with it. The other day, someone made a U-turn in the middle of the road and clearly didn't see my car coming on the opposite side. Instead of panicking or slamming on the brakes (which would've sent me into the turning car), I swerved to the right, off the road into the dirt, and then passed the car. I didn't get upset at all.

However, when I look at people, like lawyers, who spend all of their time arguing or like politicians who spend all of their time talking and shaking hands, I think to myself my unique body might very well perceive those lifestyles as stressful. I recognize that others have bodies that perceive those lifestyles as energizing and would hate sitting in a chair and putting clients into a state of hypnosis. So, knowing and accepting oneself exactly as one is is the most important factor in eliminating stress.

STRESS FROM OVERWORK AND EXHAUSTION

Depending on your personal and financial situation, the stress that results from overwork and exhaustion may or may not be avoidable. Sometimes, we just have to do what we have to do. Life is not what we expect, and our subconscious just doesn't like it. For example, a contemporary husband, who works freelance, contracts a long-term illness. He needs to rest, but he and his wife must take care of their three kids between the ages of 2 and 6. She can't support the family on her salary alone.

In this case, hypnosis can teach the father to relax and/or sleep fairly instantaneously. So, when the client is able to take a break, that break is productive and restorative. It can also help the client adjust expectations - to be more present, focusing on what *can* be done rather than wishing for an unrealistic change. Hypnosis could help this father of three embrace calm in the face of chaos and perhaps even find gratitude for the opportunity to grow closer to his wife and children.

Another thing that happens in times of overwork is that clients may begin to resent their own choices. After all, most often, the client has chosen to be in a particular situation. And so, hypnosis can help clients appreciate and feel gratitude toward their own life choices. It can keep the goal foremost in the client's mind. For example, a client who strives to be a successful painter feels sidetracked by having to take a 9-to-5 job to support her family. The artist may begin to wish she had never studied art or, conversely, wish she had never taken the job. With hypnosis, the client can remember that she has chosen to be in the situation. It can help her prioritize choices and respect her time. More importantly, hypnosis can help the client appreciate the inner strength and positive resources which allow her to engage in self-sacrifice and even feel gratitude towards the situation.

With the goal of being a successful artist foremost in the client's mind, she can make choices that allow every experience to support her talent and ambitions. Perhaps she researches galleries or sketches coworkers during her lunch hour. In short, hypnotherapy can turn what once felt like a grind into a pleasant, rewarding feeling of flow.

Of course, there are situations in which clients may feel overworked and exhausted because of a dominating boss or family member. In this case, hypnosis helps the client establish appropriate boundaries, stand up to the bully if necessary, or even walk away. I had a client with health issues who was afraid to go back to work after taking a health leave because she had been mistreated at her workplace. Hypnosis helped her change her attitude towards her abilities and attract the ideal job. With the stress significantly reduced, she could more easily take care of her health and follow the protocols her doctor had laid out for her. Initially, her goal was to improve her health, but soon it became apparent that her real goal was learning to set boundaries and appreciate her authentic self. Once she did that, her stress diminished, and her health improved.

Some people overwork out of fear of facing the *self*. These people avoid downtime to avoid seeing the truth, either about themselves or their relationships. Some people are in the wrong job and have been so heavily programmed by family or peers to be someone they're not that they're afraid to recognize it. Or, they might see themselves as heroes or martyrs for overworking. In all of these cases, such people are suffering from false perceptions – false perceptions of the self, their families, or their own obligations – as well as false perceptions of the consequences they could suffer from changing jobs, working a healthy number of hours, or simply having the courage to be oneself.

What's amazing about hypnotherapy is that the changes can feel relatively effortless. By re-programming perceptions in the subconscious, clients gain a new perspective – they simply see reality in a new light. So, they project to those around them a sense of self-assurance and confidence that allows everyone else to get on board. Of course, there are situations in which a partner or family member may feel threatened by the client's success. In a case like that, hypnotherapy can help the client separate, if necessary, from that person or teach the client to live with compassion for that person's fears.

The reasons for overwork and exhaustion are many and unique to each individual client. So, hypnosis ultimately connects clients to their innate values, making it easier for clients to see what they really want and what needs to be done to find more balance in life, whether it's accepting a situation or leaving it, whether it's embracing one's role in a family or changing it, whether it's setting appropriate boundaries or having the courage to live one's own truth.

STRESS STEMMING FROM FALSE PERCEPTIONS

Sometimes stress stems from the perception of a situation. One client, as a child, had a jealous parent and was punished for certain types of success. Now the child is an adult and the parent is long since dead. One would think that, once the mother was out of the picture, the client would've felt absolutely free to succeed, but in fact she harbored inner fears out of habit.

Every time this client took on public responsibility, she would get sick. She'd catch a cold or get digestive issues. She felt frustrated because she wanted to do more than take on adult responsibility; she wanted to be a public success. Yet, it became obvious even to her that she had an unconscious fear of it. Hypnosis changed her relationship to her dead parent and to herself. Moreover, it changed her perception of what success would mean to her life.

This client's stress came entirely from faulty belief systems. She believed, "If I succeed, I'll be punished." The belief system had been so ingrained that her negative response to desired activities was purely subconscious, but also very real and measurable. Watching herself fail, she created more and more faulty beliefs - like that she'd never achieve, that she wasn't worthy of success, and so forth. Hypnotherapy reversed those faulty beliefs, and she now leads a full life and enjoys being a leader in her community.

Clients experience stress from false beliefs in a wide variety of ways. Since the subconscious takes up 95% of the mind's activities, it's important to remember most of our perceptions are really interpretations. Sometimes false perceptions stem from huge trauma - like the client of one of my teachers who struggled with romantic relationships due to being raped by her father.

Sometimes false perceptions stem from repetition or peer pressure. I witnessed a close friend tell the Italian owner of an Italian restaurant (who spoke with an Italian accent no less) that the Italian food he served was not actually Italian. This friend had never been to Italy but had a wife whose great-grandparents came from there. Growing up the way he did gave him limited ideas of what Italian food should be. While the story is comical in retrospect, he felt a lot of stress from his false beliefs: he wouldn't eat the food and he angrily confronted the owner. He had expectations based on limited beliefs. If a limited belief like that causes embarrassment at the workplace or ruins a relationship, a client could use hypnotherapy to break the spell.

STRESS FROM MONEY

Money - along with sex - is a great source of stress in relationships, and the perception of one's financial situation heavily influences self-esteem. What's interesting is that it's not so much how much money we have but our perceptions of it and our relationship to it that really matter.

I know a highly successful money advisor who worked into his 80s, had a happy marriage, and an absolutely stunning multi-million-dollar home. He coincidentally retired the same month that the Covid pandemic began. Told by the government to stay home, he felt he was in prison. In fact, few people in their daily lives enjoy the kind of freedom and luxury this man had during lockdown. He had tennis courts and a swimming pool, three cars and stalls for horses. Yet, his perception was that he was in jail. He had no work, no active income stream, no clients and, forbidden to travel, no sense of adventure or flow. He bitterly complained to anyone who'd listen, while they'd inwardly chuckle at his false belief system.

The fact is, that on one level or another, we are all that man. We live in the most prosperous time in history. If there's a war or natural disaster, humanitarian organizations fly in water, food, and shelter. One of the biggest problems the poor have in the US is *obesity* - not starvation. Homeless people have cell phones. I'm not saying war isn't hell - it is. Being poor can indeed feel like a prison. And the homeless - often a euphemism for drug addicts and/or severely psychotic or schizophrenic individuals - may literally be living in a nightmarish alternate reality. But when I was a child, some Appalachian children had extended bellies symptomatic of starvation. The insane were locked away with little hope of achieving normalcy, and victims of war fled with the clothes on their backs and received little or no humanitarian aid. Whereas in our modern world, during Hurricane Katrina, some victims complained to the media that the free food and shelter they received weren't up to their standards. Their perception didn't match their expectation.

Our perception is limited to time, space, and our 5 senses. Expectation is based on previous experience and is totally a product of the subconscious. The key to prosperity is acceptance of what is and projecting goals for the future. By acceptance, I mean being present, existing in the here and now. By projection, I mean visualizing a desired outcome without being attached to it - without expectations. Since our expectations are limited by our experience, we can't imagine other possibilities. What if we can have something better than our expectations? If one expects to make $50,000 a year, one might miss out on an opportunity to make $70,000 or more. If one expects to make $50,000, one might not see that the $40,000 job may more easily lead to making $100,000 in less time.

And what if the motivations for our prosperity are either based on fear or at odds with our core values? If one fears poverty, no amount of success will satisfy the fear, and the subconscious will project poverty everywhere. If my work conflicts with my innate core values, my body, mind and spirit will suffer the consequences through illness, bitterness, cynicism and/or anger. Since I project fear and instability, I attract more of the same.

With the many examples of stress above, talk therapy is slow to create real change. Once a client's belief system is revealed as false, the solution is not so much to talk about it but to change the belief system from within the subconscious. With talk therapy alone, a client may take years to alter perceptions of the self, the family, or life events.

Using hypnosis as a tool to reverse issues surrounding stress and the perception of it requires as much time and thought as working with a complex illness. First, one must acknowledge all the behaviors, large and small, that make life appear more difficult and distasteful than it is. Second, one must go back to the times in life where those behaviors became ingrained, reverse one's relationship to those events, and discover and utilize new resources. Third, one must allow the hypnotherapist, with one's help, to help one define (or redefine) core values. Who you really are may even come as a bit of a shock to you, but you must embrace your core self; otherwise, stress remains a constant, and prosperity in any form - health, money, relationships - continues to slip away. For some, embracing their true self is a great act of faith.

4

It Reduces Pain

"Pain is inevitable; suffering is optional."

—BUDDHIST PROVERB

It's fascinating to me that so many today align themselves with ancient cultures. Even the Paleo diet movement claims inspiration from our prehistoric ancestors. I think that, surrounded by so much prosperity - especially in the form of technology - modern people are drawn to the values of the ancient simply to gain some perspective on what really matters.

As much as the Dalai Lama wears glasses, speaks at stadiums, and flies first class, he grew up in a place that had no lights, toilets, dentists, or surgeons. As a youth, he experienced pain and loss as part of everyday life; moreover, he knew others experienced the same pain and loss. That perspective is lacking in the post-iPhone world where dental patients are encouraged to take opioids after even minor dental work or surgeries. I have heard a few people as old as 65 say they've never experienced pain or disappointment – outside of the occasional scraped knee. Of course, such inexperienced people can lack empathy for those who do feel pain; but more importantly, these people, not having experienced it, can be unreasonably afraid of pain and vulnerable when experiencing it.

If you are human, at some point in your life you are likely to experience serious pain. From the hypnosis perspective, there are three kinds of physical pain: acute, systemic, and chronic. People may also feel physical pain with respect to grief and depression. Acute pain is pretty straightforward: that's the kind of pain that gets better when the source of pain is removed or heals. It ranges from boo-boos to broken arms to abscessed teeth and gunshot wounds. Systemic pain, as the name implies, means pain that courses through your whole system – that kind of pain is often associated with an infection or virus. It can also result as a side effect of a medication, drug or food poisoning. A hangover might give you a good dose of systemic pain. Some conditions like diabetes or autoimmune disease can affect the nervous system and, hence, create a sensation of full body pain. Chronic pain is the most puzzling of all. It occurs on its own after an extended period of acute or systemic pain. Apparently, parts of the brain that process pain become taken over by the constant, repeated experience of pain until pain is simply a reality.[11] All types of pain can be improved through the practice of hypnosis.

Fortunately (or unfortunately) for myself, I have experienced two of the three types of physical pain - acute and systemic, and my husband has experienced all three. Not only have I broken bones and have had a couple abscessed teeth, but during a near-fatal accident I felt pain so deep and profound it's difficult to describe. I can only say that if someone else has experienced that same level of pain, as my husband has, that person knows what I'm talking about.

By that time, I was a hypnotherapist and so I knew doing self-hypnosis during the very long journey to life-saving surgery, as well as during the painful recovery, would reduce the effects of trauma. My memory of the entire ordeal includes pain only at key points, like when the pain first began and I recognized I could die, or once I tried to walk again before my ribs and back had fully healed from the trauma. But because I did self-hypnosis throughout the process - on the way to the hospital, the week I was in the hospital, and frequently during the two months it took me to walk comfortably again - I don't have much memory of pain. I remember the self-hypnosis, and I think that's why I managed to avoid chronic pain.

---

[11] Doidge, N., M.D. (2015). *The Brain's Way of Healing* (p. Chapter1). Viking, an Imprint of Penguin Group.

In general, clients don't come to hypnotherapy for acute pain because acute pain is often so short-lived. When the source of the pain is removed, the pain vanishes. However, knowledge and experience with hypnosis can really help an individual suffering from acute pain. Basically, acute pain can be made manageable by simply distracting the brain. Perhaps you remember as a child having chickenpox or a rash and being given toys and puzzles to keep your mind off the pain. With hypnosis, one can dive into the realm of the subconscious and create a range of sensory experiences so pleasurable that the pain itself can be much diminished or even vanish entirely. Doing so can prevent a situation in which chronic pain could manifest. So, for example, when I was being airlifted to Colorado, the pain was extreme – really indescribable. Because I put myself in another, very pleasurable place and time, my memories of the event are mixed, and the memories of my pain are minimal. Those who truly master the art of self-hypnosis can use hypnosis in place of anesthesia for much greater potential experiences of pain, as in childbirth or at the dentist's office.

Having rheumatoid arthritis, I occasionally experience systemic pain. Interestingly, I've found that systemic pain is often triggered by a psychological experience. For example, if I'm working too hard and feel pressured to succeed, that puts pressure on my nervous system, and then suddenly I'll begin to experience nerve pain in my hands and feet. An arthritis flare, for me, is usually preceded by a bout of anger.

Even those stomach pains that accompany a virus might be triggered by a psychological experience or event. For example, someone who experiences a sudden disappointment or trauma might be more likely to catch the flu. So, in cases with a clear psychological trigger, a client can access hypnosis in order to reverse the triggers. When I recognized that my experience of rheumatoid arthritis was directly linked to emotions and fatigue, I used hypnotherapy to a) address the deep underlying reasons for the triggers, and b) encourage new habits to prevent recurrences.

All chronic pain patients would benefit, even to some degree, from hypnotherapy. This is because chronic pain is basically a habit. It's almost like an addiction for the parts of the brain that process pain.[12] With hypnosis, the client can create new pathways in the brain and a new relationship to the areas of the brain that process pain. For example, my husband had a near-death experience with the same level of extreme pain I felt during my near-fatal accident. After the ICU, he acquired a lasting infection. Not having the benefit of hypnosis, or even psychiatric counseling (which I did ask the hospital to provide), his experience was, quite simply, extreme pain and/or the side effects of various pain meds, which included constipation (more pain) and hallucinations (more trauma.)

Of course, my husband acquired chronic pain, and until he did hypnosis, he was in pain for years. Physically, he still experiences some pain because he has troubled vertebrae in his neck and back. But the chronic, exhausting, never-one-moment-of-peace type of pain vanished thanks to various hypnotic techniques.

There were multiple layers to the hypnotherapy he received. First, he handled the chronic pain by imagining a healthy brain. That sounds simple, but it involves great discipline. Every time he experienced chronic pain, he imagined his brain healthy again. The sole goal of this exercise was not to relieve the pain itself.

---

[12] Doidge, N., M.D. (2015). *The Brain's Way of Healing* (p. Chapter1). Viking, an Imprint of Penguin Group.

The goal was to heal his brain so that his brain real estate was no longer taken over by pain. The reason that pain relief is not the goal is that imagining pain triggers those pathways in the brain that are already damaged. Therefore, the goal had to be making the brain healthy again.

That technique worked almost instantly, though when I learned about it, I understood that the technique could take many months before the client would see results. Next, he did approaches that would diminish some of his acute pain. They mostly involved some form of mental imagery.

Most importantly, he worked on reversing limited beliefs through traditional hypnotherapy techniques like regression. The reason for this was that he had psychological distress at the time of his surgery. He had had trauma at work, trauma in his extended family, and enormous change in our personal family life. Part of him wanted to die. Since he didn't, and life was riddled with pain, he was left with no choice but to address the reasons why.

The fact that psychological trauma and stress usually surround a client's initial experience of chronic pain is extremely common. It is almost as if the trauma creates a weakness in the client - in the body or in the mind – that makes acquiring an illness or having an accident more likely. In any case, chronic pain itself is so psychologically debilitating that some form of psychological healing is often necessary to heal the pain. Talk therapy is definitely not the way to do this. By talking about pain, the client stimulates centers of the brain that process pain, and the pain remains. Hypnosis can simultaneously heal those parts of the brain and reverse the trauma and negative belief systems that contributed to the problem in the first place.

I had a client who was born with one kidney, and at this point in his life had been on dialysis for several years. His wise goal was not to completely heal the situation but to walk and stand better, since the natural results of one kidney and being on dialysis for so long meant that he was acquiring osteoporosis and had considerable back pain. In the course of his six sessions, we discovered something important: that when he was diagnosed as a little boy, he understandably didn't like being in the hospital, and his parents understandably told him that the doctors were always right. This false belief no longer serves an accomplished 67-year-old man. It created a sense of dependency – a sense that the body itself might not know the answer.

The best doctor/patient relationships come when there is a kind of partnership. A good patient inspires the doctor to do his or her level best. A good patient walks away from doctors who don't give their best. A good doctor has humility about the limitations of what is possible. Rediscovering independence was one of the affirmations my client chose. Although this man will go to doctors for the rest of his life, freeing himself from the false belief - that doctors are always right - returned this man to independence. He stopped using his canes.

Pain is a complex issue, indeed. While it's certainly true that the best way to eliminate pain from a splinter is to remove the splinter, it's also true that a client can cope with that pain better, and even outright eliminate it, with the help of hypnosis. The discovery that chronic pain is manufactured by the brain itself reveals the mind's power to heal. If imagining an event triggers similar responses in the body and brain to exposure to the event itself, then using the imagination to reverse trauma is simply common sense. Chronic pain is not just debilitating to the body, it literally robs the brain of its ability to think, focus, and enjoy life. Naturally, chronic pain sufferers would do anything for an immediate fix – and medication can seem like the best path. But because chronic pain is really about the brain's false perceptions, medication does not always fill the bill. Hypnosis not only helps the brain ally with reality, it can also inspire the brain to come up with solutions that doctors might not have thought of.

It Contributes
to Self-Healing

"The process of self-healing is the privilege of every being. Self-healing is not a miracle, nor is self-healing a dramatization of the personality as though you could do something superior. Self-healing is a genuine process of the relationship between the physical and the infinite power of the soul."

—HARBHAJAN SINGH YOGI

"We are not victims of our genes, but masters of our fates, able to create lives overflowing with peace, happiness, and love."

—BRUCE H. LIPTON, The Biology of Belief:
Unleashing the Power of Consciousness, Matter and Miracles

Helping clients heal themselves is probably the most important thing that a hypnotherapist can do. I believe that human beings have an almost infinite capacity to heal themselves – but time and know-how conspire to prevent miracles from happening.

One of my hypnotherapy teachers was a woman who experienced enormous physical trauma as a young adult. While crossing an intersection in her car, she was broadsided by an 18-wheeler. This happened about 30 years ago in South America. Medical care in that place and time was not as advanced as it is now. After the examination at the hospital, they sent her home to die. But she didn't die. She couldn't walk on her own, go to the bathroom on her own, or see. Her skull was crushed. As part of our training, she showed us students her x-rays. They were scary to see.

My teacher came from a wealthy family, however, so a relative continued to help, network, and research. Eventually she came upon a neurosurgeon, hoping that the man could operate and restore her sister's head shape and brain function. The man turned out to also be a hypnotherapist. He went to my teacher's house to see her in person. So much time had passed since the accident, that he feared that more surgery would be yet another trauma and might not yield the healing everyone hoped for. So, in addition to doing hypnotherapy with my teacher personally, he also created hypnosis recordings for her to listen to. Basically, she listened to them 24 hours a day for many months. The results were absolutely miraculous. Today, she is in her late 50s, stunningly beautiful, and amazingly brilliant. One has to look very closely to see any signs of the accident.

I have my own theories about why and how this miracle occurred. First, I know from personal experience that, when one is both near death and in that much pain, the conscious mind goes almost blank. In fact, being near death is about the closest I've ever come to being completely in the moment. Each breath is another "now." So, that means my teacher may have resisted very little. Her mind would've been completely open, and not being able to move, she had little choice.

More importantly, my teacher had all the time in the world to listen to these recordings. She was completely open and available in a way that few people could ever be. So, when the doctor included suggestions that her bones might move to their natural, healthy placement, they did – slowly and gradually over many months. Her eyesight returned. Her digestion normalized. In short, without any medicines or surgeries, her body healed itself with his guidance.

In what ways did the doctor guide her? Some of his suggestions were purely biological – asking bits of her body to go back to where they once were and/or resume their natural function. Some of his suggestions reversed the trauma she had just experienced. Some worked on her as an individual, to reverse negative belief systems and instill positive ones. Collectively, they did the trick. And her diligent, loving family did all the physical work: they fed and bathed her, they helped her walk and move, and most importantly they believed hypnotherapy would work and provided daily support for it.

My teacher's story is remarkable, but she is not alone.

Neuroscientist and self-help guru Joe Dispenza, D.C., broke his back at age 26. At the time, he worked as a chiropractor. Hearing his prognosis, and recognizing that the surgeons giving him advice did not understand the spine much better than he did, he left the hospital and used his mind to heal himself. He recounts his story - and those of myriad others - in his various books on the mind, including You Are the Placebo: Making Your Mind Matter.[13] Rather like my teacher, he spent many hours every day for months projecting his body to heal. He got so engaged that he could tell by fractions of seconds whether his mind was focused and whether negative thinking crept into his mind.

Obviously, Dr. Joe's back healed. But his success launched a new career for him as a researcher undertaking the task of proving how he succeeded. He partners with other research organizations such as the Heartmath Institute,[14] University of California San Diego, Australia's Bond University Department of Psychology, and the University of Auckland Department of Neuroscience and Psychology.[15]

When I was 13, my mother had a "nervous breakdown" for which she was given shock therapy. I put those words in quotes because years later, when I learned about alternative medicine, I realized my hunches as a young adult were correct: she had been misdiagnosed. Once I was old enough to drive, I escorted my mother to therapy because she would be too upset to drive on the way back. We would talk about her sessions, which was inappropriate, but that allowed me to observe patterns in her life

that told me talk therapy wasn't going to do her that much good

[13] Dispenza, Joe. You Are the Placebo: Making Your Mind Matter. Hay House, Inc., 2018.
[14] https://www.heartmath.org
[15] https://drjoedispenza.com/blogs/research

- nor would the drugs she eventually took for the rest of her life.

What I saw, even as a young adult, was a combination of bad diet, inactive lifestyle, heredity, and - most importantly - false negative perceptions of herself and the world. The therapists she saw over 25 years really did nothing but reinforce those negative beliefs, many of which had become outright false once she was in her 40s and married to a successful man. She thought of herself as poor, for example, because she grew up in the Depression. She kept thinking my father would die the way her father did, when in fact he outlived her by 20 years. I wished some of these doctors would have pointed out that what was keeping her back were simply perceptions inspired by subconscious programming. She had the capacity to heal herself, but back in the 1970s and 80s, no one ever suggested anything as simple as altering her diet. She trusted her doctors, and so her various doctors' negative prognoses became her reality.

I have autoimmune disease, and so the fact that I lead a busy, productive life demonstrates the importance of a positive mindset. If I become angry, if I become overwrought, if I doubt myself, the likelihood of my experiencing a flare-up rises. This reality has caused me, over time, to implement various tools - with hypnosis and meditation ranking at the top - to keep my attitude positive.

Just as with chronic pain, negative emotions and false beliefs can make in-roads in the brain, even taking up areas of the brain meant for other purposes. By living more in the moment, these in-roads go away or never get formed. And, hypnotherapy also helps keep me living in the moment. The present moment is often beautiful and stress-free. Experiencing friends or being in nature keeps the spirit uplifted, and medically stimulates the parasympathetic nervous system. If I'm watching the news, my heart might start beating faster or I may become irritated. Turning off the television, I'm just here in my living room. No one is attacking me. No one expects anything of me. I can just be. It takes a little bit of discipline to separate yourself from gossip or current events, but doing so, you will probably find staying informed is less time consuming and less emotional. When intuition and common sense start taking over, the body feels more aligned with reality.

Sometimes, people just don't want to heal. As I've said, hypnotherapy does not work for people who don't want it to work. If you don't believe in it, I can't make you. If you are cynical during treatment, you won't experience the benefits to the extent you would if you were positive. Part of you will always be saying, "I knew it wouldn't work," even if you begin to experience improvement. It's interesting how many husbands come in because their wives make them and want to show her how foolish she is, or how many addicts are looking for yet another way to prove that recovering from addiction is hopeless. A client may consciously believe they want to heal; but their subconscious does everything it can to get in the way of healing. Until such people can accept responsibility for all of their behaviors – even the unconscious, compulsive or accidental ones - true healing is less likely to happen.

People who shun healing have often experienced deep shame in their lives. Some of them don't want to heal because they don't feel they deserve it. Compassion for the self is just one cure for shame; hypnotherapy can help you have that compassion, and as a result, completely let go of unwanted behavior.

Talk therapy might actually benefit the reluctant client more than hypnosis, simply because the talk therapist may gradually get the client to see the need for taking responsibility for every breath of life. But for clients with physical or mental issues who recognize that an improved attitude is the best starting point for true recovery, hypnosis is the way to go.

In the self-healing process, clients sometimes realize that their true goal is not the goal they came in with. For example, I had a client whose goal was to improve his public speaking. He did public speaking all the time, yet suddenly he felt self-conscious. After several sessions, it became apparent that he felt self-conscious because he allowed the criticisms of a co-worker to influence him. Then, it became apparent that the man had poor boundaries in many areas of his life; this is why he took the co-worker's comments so much to heart. The comments weren't perceived as constructive criticism; they were perceived as a personal attack. Whether or not the comments were meant as an attack is irrelevant; this man allowed the comments to destroy his performance. So, he had to be open to finding out why, at his age, he was so vulnerable. This rabbit hole went deeper and ultimately ended with false ideas he accepted about himself as a little boy and child of an alcoholic. The fact that the client was willing to keep unraveling the onion with me shows his personal courage and dedication to his profession. He really wanted to heal and could tell at every stage he had more work to do. His ability to be honest with himself meant that he could heal.

As a writer for the stage, I learned to take my audience from A to B with my words. Now, with my clients - my audiences of one - I use my intention, my skill, and my words, to establish another state of mind - one of positivity and self-healing that is drawn entirely from the client's own desires. I had gone into acting while my mother was having her "breakdown" largely because, compared to home, the stage was a safe place in which to express myself. I found that, contrary to the beliefs of those with stage fright, the stage was the safest place to be in the world. There, I could be myself and that, all by itself, was healing for me. So now I create an environment in my healing sessions where any and every emotion the client expresses is welcome and accepted, and where the client experiences the story of his or her own life from a new, healing perspective.

Believing in a positive future and accepting yourself are, in my view, the two most important placebos for transforming your life and, yes, for healing yourself. Not that this is always easy. Recounting his healing journey, Dr. Joe reflects on the negative mindset he had at the outset. If your doctor tells you that you will never walk again, you would be silly not to take that seriously. And to stay positive during and after that conversation takes a level of courage that few have without outside support.

The body is designed to heal itself. If we get a cold or a scrape, the body marshals its forces. Although it's true that some enjoy more robust constitutions than others, the mind is key to healing success. If a patient does not believe it's possible to heal, healing is more difficult or takes more time. If a patient has subconscious blocks that steer the patient away from healing, healing will be a challenge. If the mind is open to healing and learning from the experience of illness, healing to some extent will happen in even the most dire circumstances. If a client has terminal cancer, for example, spontaneous remission may be possible, but it's not likely. Yet, a patient with the belief that life is worth living, that every challenge is secretly a gift, that cancer is nothing but an experience on a life journey in which everyone dies at the end, that patient will live well until the end and die well when death comes - and occasionally, the peace that comes with that mindset can trigger remission.

There's a saying, "Living well is the best revenge," because so few people do it. Life really isn't about having money or status or doing the right or wrong things by society's standards; a good life means feeling at peace with decisions, emotions, and relationships. As famed psychotherapist Milton Erickson said, "Life will bring you pain all by itself. Your responsibility is to create joy." Creating joy is self-healing at its best.

It Restores Faith and the Courage to Live in Faith

"Faith is passionate intuition."

—WILLIAM WORDSWORTH

The real power of hypnotherapy rests in stimulating the superconscious of the client. Remember that the superconscious is largely measurable when a client is in alpha and theta states, and that human beings experience the superconscious as a connection to God, a higher power, or a higher self. According to Ran D. Anbar, M.D. in a 2021 Psychology Today article, "Becoming aware of the great power of the subconscious mind through hypnosis can lead to enhanced spiritual understanding." It also gives clients perspective and can even clarify their purpose in life.[16]

In my practice, I have met every kind of believer and even those who believe in disbelieving. Atheists may not believe in God, but they do have a name for this higher power state. Whether they call it the Source, flow, Nature, or gratitude, they have the capacity to experience the superconscious just as much as people who believe in Christ, Mohammed, or Buddha. In her book Future Memory,[17] near-death experience researcher and author PMH Atwater describes not only near-death experiences but also a phenomenon in which individuals experience what she calls "future memory," that is, they have visions of the future that are more solid and specific than déjà vu, and which come true.

Tying her research to that of others, Atwater theorizes a link between the human experience of God and quantum physics. The idea is that the superconscious is actually the human link to a kind of universal intelligence. According to Atwater, our intuition is something slightly more than our experience merged with our intelligence; it's a connection between people and the entire universe.

---

[16] https://www.psychologytoday.com/us/blog/understanding-hypnosis/202112/spirituality-and-hypnosis
[17] Atwater, PMH. *Future Memory*. Hampton Roads., 2013.

After college, I went into the theater professionally and that trained me to speak and carry myself well. But more importantly, it taught me about the invisible connection between people. One actor on stage can control the emotions of an audience of thousands. And, as I learned, all that was necessary to win over an audience was for the actor to have a strong intention and concentration.

The actor could sit still, doing nothing, but if the intention and concentration were strong enough, the audience would be riveted. I saw almost immediately that there was a kind of healing in the projection of strong, positive intentions. So, as a hypnotherapist, my intention is to heal, and my clients feel that. When they've completed their sessions, they usually discover their intentions (to sleep well, eat better, succeed at work, get along with someone) have borne fruit.

Former chiropractor turned neuroscience researcher Dr. Joe Dispenza is also doing research on the mind-body-spirit connection and how the superconscious can be employed to heal the human experience.[18] Employing EEG devices, he and his research team have shown how the brain literally improves functionality when the mind accesses the superconscious. A brain stressed with what Dispenza describes as scattered impulses suddenly transforms itself in meditation or trance states into organized impulses when a subject "connects with source." He claims this gamma brain wave state has resulted in physical healing in the bodies of some of his subjects.[19]

---

[18] https://drjoedispenza.com/pages/scientific-research
[19] Dispenza, Joe. *Becoming Supernatural*. HAY HOUSE UK LTD, 2017.

Perhaps someday we will prove with measurable accuracy what God is and our relationship to it. Who knows? In the meantime, I believe it is highly valuable to cultivate a relationship with the superconscious by relating to some higher power. A minister came to my house and commented on my altar - which featured Jesus, Mary, Buddha and a couple other entities - that I was "covering a lot of bases." But in fact, my altar simply represents my spiritual journey. I grew up Catholic, I discovered meditation, I'm a certified kundalini yoga teacher and more. I feel that my experiments with spirituality have made me an exceptionally valuable servant to others in reconnecting to their faith, whether they are hard-core atheists, religious zealots, or representatives of some shade of gray in between.

Even though I'm a Christian, I have enough knowledge of comparative religion to respect everyone's belief system. I know that most religious texts simply describe in story or verse what the eastern religions called "duality," that is the separation between God and man. Sometimes these texts describe higher states of consciousness. Christ's death, for example, is referred to as "the passion," a higher state of consciousness in which, through his death and resurrection, he ultimately merges back with God the Father. I have enough personal experience with higher states of consciousness to know that they matter. We all have faith of some kind, and to be disconnected from it is a frightening experience for any human being.

In this context, I'm not speaking of religion. I'm really talking about a deep connection to one's own soul. I have practiced Kundalini Yoga daily for 27 years now. I find that the practice deeply connects me to my soul and, of course, helps me be a better hypnotherapist. However, over the years, I've been sometimes amused, sometimes disturbed by the reactions I get from people when I say I do yoga - not even Kundalini Yoga – just plain yoga, for there are some religious people who still in this day and age think that yoga is a threat to their faith. Wouldn't it be true that, if their belief was strong enough, surely it would withstand a little "downward dog"? Wouldn't an experiment in something new reveal something more true about these individuals and their connection to their own souls than not experimenting at all?

Similarly, my husband used to work with scientists. Many of these same people, whose views were allegedly grounded in science and experimentation, just couldn't handle people with different points of view. Some didn't particularly see people as having souls. More likely they thought of people as having brains, which, believe it or not, some would have liked to have transferred into the hard drive of a computer. The quest for science for many of these people was really a masquerade to protect their own fragile belief systems. On the other hand, I found that the most brilliant scientists we came across were actually extremely open-minded; they could accept pretty much any point of view because they acknowledged that science is an eternal work in progress. These geniuses, whether or not they had a religious faith, had a great faith in science. They lived by the beauty of it and respected, if not cherished, the unknown.

I've come to realize that a connection to faith equals a connection to the unknown and a connection to life's purpose. The adventure of life can only expand and inform your faith — that is, unless you are attached to false belief systems and ideals. In trance, the true self – the superconscious (some might say *the soul)* emerges and speaks its truth. Most of the time, clients experience a great epiphany when they reconnect with this part of themselves. Occasionally, individuals are so attached to their social image or their need to be right, that they reject themselves. These people are not good candidates for hypnotherapy unless they decide to work on the part of themselves that isn't at home in their own skin.

Talk therapy does little to address faith - religious or otherwise. In fact, I would recommend that those seeking talk therapy find a therapist who shares their religious beliefs. That way, a client wouldn't have to discuss faith at all; it would be an inherently understood element of the client's healing. And both therapist and client would understand it in exactly the same way.

As I've said before, even someone who doesn't believe in God does have a higher self – it's a measurable brain state. And, it can take months and months of talking for the therapist to even have a glimmer of the client's *soul* purpose. Worse, a therapist with a differing belief system might actually spend a good amount of time trying to convince a client that their core values and desires are just plain wrong. Whereas, in hypnosis, the soul reveals itself pretty quickly. The only trouble that can occur is when a hypnotherapist is personally at odds with that soul.

One early client was a successful retired woman, who had reinvented herself as an artist. She was also a lesbian, and she and her former partner had used a sperm bank to conceive her son. As a young adult, her son tragically died in a motor vehicle accident. My client came to me for weight loss, and very quickly it became apparent that she had two obstacles preventing her progress: first, grieving her son was her way of connecting to him, so she was afraid to stop grieving; and second, she had spent a lifetime wearing a psychological mask.

This client put on a happy face for people; and very few knew her real demeanor, let alone the depths of her suffering. Sure enough, in trance, she began to weep. And she hated it. Soon, she told me the whole truth about her son. But then she hated having told me. She also shared her political beliefs. She held a host of narrow, uninformed opinions that kept her from feeling comfortable around most people. After a few sessions, we parted ways because she literally would not let go of her mask even one-on-one. She had absolutely no faith in herself, let alone faith in God, spirit, Nature or anything higher.

Another client - a young woman in her 30s – had a very rare autoimmune disease that got triggered when she was working in an emotionally toxic corporate environment. Having worked in corporations for all of her young career, this young woman also wore a psychological mask. In contrast, when I asked her if she'd like to get rid of it, she answered a resounding "yes." This woman had close family and friends who loved her and, though not exactly religious, she believed in God. The young woman knew that discovering her core self might mean changing her lifestyle – and that change might disrupt the family she loved. Yet, she had faith that they would ultimately accept her positive growth and that more than anything they wanted her to be healthy.

Comparing the two clients, one can see that the older woman was unwilling to surrender her ego. She had no spiritual beliefs at all - she didn't even connect spiritually with nature - plus she had no support network, even though she knew a lot of people. The older woman had had a traumatic childhood and trusted no one - not even members of her own family. On the other hand, the young woman surrendered - to the sessions, to her idea of God, and to her unknown future. She completed her treatment and began a wonderful new job in a warm, welcoming work environment. She found she could be successful and get the support she needed from her employers to maintain her own health. The older woman quit treatment because she was so attached to her negative way of being, and she felt uncomfortable when she tried to let it go. Faith might've given her the strength to transform.

Hypnosis restores faith by revealing the superconscious – the soul – to the client. If the client is ready to embrace the core self, hypnosis can work deeply and quickly on almost any issue, even lifetime problems. By connecting to that higher universal intelligence, the client experiences a sense of flow and connection to the present. It's suddenly OK to be here now, standing on this earth, dealing with life's problems. Life is experience, and much of our experience comes from problems or negative situations. If we accept that simple premise of living and dealing with things until we die, then faith in ourselves returns and supports us on our life's journey.

7

It Provides Excellent Medical Support

"The strength of the placebo response can be of any magnitude. It can relieve severe postoperative pain, induce sleep or mental alertness, ... In addition, recent research has shown that the placebo response can occur even when patients are completely aware that they're getting the equivalent of the sugar pill."

—ANDREW WEIL

The word placebo holds the connotation of a false solution. Actually, however, the fact that placebos can deliver amazing results and even, in some cases, cure the physical body, simply shows the power of the mind. If you have ever known an old person on the verge of death live to see a baby born, a graduation, or a wedding, you have seen the power of placebo. The sense of hope and love literally fills the ailing body with a kind of healing magic. How it works doesn't really matter. What matters is that every cell of the body gets the message, and the seemingly impossible - a few more weeks of life - occurs.

The placebo effect is well known and scientifically measurable. In fact, Harvard University offers a Program in Placebo Studies and Therapeutic Encounter.[20] Harvard has studied hypnosis as part of this program. Harvard's Irving Kirsch wrote a paper called "Clinical Hypnosis as a Nondeceptive Placebo."[21]The idea is that hypnosis can create such a positive mindset and such a strong belief in recovery that, like placebos used in place of a test drug in a clinical study, patients get better. It's "nondeceptive" because patients know they are receiving it. The article shows how "many psychological problems are maintained by 'dysfunctional response expectancies.'" Changing these expectations to positive and functional substantially enhances psychotherapy's effects.

While placebos give a positive effect; *nocebos* create negative effects. Nocebos are a kind of "dysfunctional response expectancy." An example of a nocebo might be a doctor telling a patient he will die in a few days, and the patient dies within a few minutes. Nocebos are examples of negative programming. If we

20 http://programinplacebostudies.org/
21 https://psycnet.apa.org/record/1995-14577-001

believe something bad will happen, it may very well happen. If we have been programmed to fear illness instead of learn from it, we will probably stay sick longer than expected. If we carry an image in our mind of the kind of person we are or of how life should go, our bodies will likely manifest it. Hypnosis is an excellent tool for reversing nocebos or other types of negative belief systems, and that's why it's an excellent tool for medical support.

One of the purposes of my life seems to be to experience something physical and scary (illness, accidents, surgery), discover the best ways to deal with it, and then spread the word. I'm not always happy about this piece of karma. But I am happy over the number of people I've helped in my life as a result, especially once I became a hypnotherapist. It's unusual to perceive a lifetime of illness as a blessing. I have scoliosis and mitral valve prolapse, which were diagnosed when I was 13 and 17 respectively - and both, as I learned in my subsequent studies, heavily influenced my health, immune system, and perceptions. I have had rheumatoid arthritis for 35 years, Hashimoto's thyroiditis for 8, and the occasional bout of collagenous colitis. The RA ate away at a joint on my right wrist, which became sharp enough to cut through a tendon. This meant I had to have my hand reconstructed. At the time, I was 35 with a small child. Since it was obvious that what the doctors were doing wasn't working for me, that event launched me on my discovery of alternative healing methods.

At that point, I also came to see how much our emotional states influence health. By the time I was 40, I'd say that I had acquired a positive mindset for recovering from whatever my body threw at me. Although that didn't entirely stop illness from happening, it improved the quality of life to a remarkable extent, and it allowed me to learn how to turn negative situations into positive, as well as learn from them.

My experience that mindset can reduce symptoms and even induce healing is backed up by studies on wound healing. One conducted by Harvard Medical School in conjunction with the Union Institute in Cincinnati showed that hypnosis helps people feel better physically, and it helps "the mind make structural changes in the body, accelerating healing at the tissue level." In another study conducted by Harvard at Massachusetts General Hospital in Boston, hypnotized patients with broken ankles healed more quickly than the control group. In fact, those in the hypnosis group at six weeks after the fracture showed the equivalent of eight and a half weeks of healing without.[22]

In my own healing journey, I learned the power of the subconscious is vast and can induce illness as well as healing. Human beings have a purpose, if not a destiny, and if they are not true to that purpose, illness may very well hunt them down. Canadian physician Gabor Maté has researched and written about this phenomenon in his book When the Body Says No: The Cost of Hidden Stress. In it, he describes similarities he's observed between patients suffering from a similar disease. For example, he drew conclusions about the suppressed anger experienced by those with autoimmune disease, or the compulsive caretaking and sacrifice of ALS sufferers. He shows that if a child's early years are fraught with doubt or abuse, the child may expect that the doubt and abuse will remain. However, many who leave a life of abuse behind may find that the trauma will represent itself through disease.[23]

[22] https://news.harvard.edu/gazette/story/2003/05/hypnosis-helps-healing-2/
[23] Gabor Maté. When the Body Says No: The Cost of Hidden Stress. Vermilion, 2019

In regard to my own life, I did indeed suffer from the repressed anger Maté claims autoimmune sufferers experienced. Once I found meditation and changed my mindset, I achieved a remarkable 14-year, drug-free remission from rheumatoid arthritis. During that period of time, I not only took the right supplements and did the right exercise, but I was also happy. I was happy raising my children and, in my marriage, because my husband was happy with his work. But then, things changed fairly quickly. My husband got a new boss who made him miserable. My children became teenagers and left home. Family members and friends started dying – we lost 13 people in a period of 18 months. Society changed in ways too numerous to mention, and that put pressure on my theater business. I felt like I was running ahead of a train, even though I was doing all the things I loved to do. Eventually, a tourist ran a red light and struck my car on the driver's side. I received a concussion that took eight months to recover from. The shock of the accident on my system pushed me into instant menopause. I wound up selling my business because, with the rate the world was changing, I just couldn't keep up. It was that or go into mounds of debt.

Basically, the equilibrium I had experienced for 14 years vanished; anger, frustration, and illness returned. Not only did the rheumatoid arthritis come back, but I acquired Hashimoto's thyroiditis and eventually collagenous colitis. Everyone, including my doctors, was encouraging me to go the natural route to regain remission because I had had remission seemingly mere moments before. But the fact is, there was a lot to unravel – emotionally as well as physically. The process just took time. The good thing about it was that I did have the proper mindset for healing. I was ready to look at anything, and I did. Interestingly, I discovered hypnosis at this time. The practitioner really didn't know how to go about unraveling all the psychological influences that surrounded my relapse. But I recognized that, in hypnotherapy, I had found a solution.

So, what needed to be unpacked? 1. The mountains of grief my husband and I were experiencing from losing so many friends and loved ones. 2. The fact that my husband was now miserable in his work and bringing his misery home. On my end, I didn't know how to help or support him. And the situation gave us financial pressure. 3. While I loved doing the work of my business, the business environment had simply changed. This business was not going to be viable or enjoyable anymore. That realization was heartbreaking, and made me feel adrift. Why did I achieve so much only for it to be taken away? 4. I had had a concussion and whiplash in my neck and back. In the process of seeking care for it, I received a lot of nocebos and general bad advice from unreliable doctors and health practitioners. I was healing myself again, and that made me feel resentful and frightened.

How would I treat myself, as a hypnotherapist, if I was presented with such a case? First, I would reverse the doctors' nocebos and give the client recordings to listen to multiple times a day that would support rebuilding the back, neck, and brain. This would be easy for the client to execute because she (I) literally couldn't move for a while, and it would be a long time before she (I) could even drive again. These kinds of recordings consist of deep relaxation and symbolic instructions to the body to heal in very specific ways.

Second, I would reverse the trauma of the accident itself. I would help this client feel comfortable in a car again. Third, I would work on her relationship with her husband so that the pressure on him from her illness would be diminished. By altering her expectations of how her husband needs to be acting at this time, she would become more self-sufficient, and he would feel less threatened while he sorted out his own relationship to his job.

Fourth, I would help the client discover and/or embrace her life's purpose. By putting the accident in context with a higher goal, the accident becomes a gift and a learning experience rather than a source of suffering. If the client was not me but someone who hasn't had a lot of experience with illness, I would help that client embrace the challenging protocols of healing – the new supplements, diet, the brain exercises, the rest, every necessary thing that feels difficult or unpleasant to do. I might have to take my client back to her childhood to learn what is obstructing her healing and perhaps to discover resources that could support her present healing. All of this would take at least 10 sessions. It might feel like a financial burden at the time, but the payoff would be worth it because the client would return to health sooner, and that means work again sooner, and there would be less strain on the marriage.

Going to talk therapy was simply not an option for a very long time after the accident. I literally couldn't do it - couldn't talk for an hour, couldn't drive there. By the time I could do something like that, there would be even more psychological stuff to unpack. Then, of course, it would take three months just to get to know me. Although many people do go to therapy after an extreme trauma like that, the risk is that talking about it just reinforces the mental images that caused the fear, resentment, and anger.

At some point, my husband might've been dragged in there to discuss how unhappy he was at work. He had made a decision to stay and deal with the unpleasant environment, so talking about it, again, might not have been useful in dealing with it. Whereas, if he had done hypnosis himself at that time, he might've felt more at peace with his choice or made a different choice with confidence. And of course, the therapist would expect a commitment of years. In contrast, a thoughtful hypnotherapist would address the problem in pieces, first supporting the body in recovery, and then in an appropriate time frame, supporting the mind. Ten sessions is an expense, but spreading it out and breaking the problem down into pieces would make the solution affordable and effective.

I had a client who asked me to help prepare her for back surgery. She had had other surgeries before and was in terrible pain when she stood or sat. In terms of being a patient, she had several issues. One was that she didn't feel confident talking to doctors. She would let them speak and then do whatever they told her to do, even if she disagreed with it. She didn't want to "waste their time." She didn't want to be a bother.

This woman had the same attitude when it came to asking people to help or take care of her. She resented them because she felt she was a bother to them. We did much to prepare her mentally for the practical physical steps of the surgery and recovering from it, and we even prepared for the possibility of not getting the surgery at all. However, the biggest thing we did to prepare her was to take her back to the first moment she felt she was a bother to someone.

It turned out that being a bother was the impression that the client got from her father growing up. He said she wasted other people's time. Even though she described the man as loving in every other respect, those were words he had used. So, by reversing that trauma and giving her new resources, she was able to stop thinking of herself as a bother, or at least recognize that if she thought she was a bother it was just her subconscious programming. As a result, she began engaging in practical discussions with her doctor and his staff. She learned to be gracious in her questioning and appreciate that they wanted to succeed in their work. If she came across physicians who did not show her respect by answering her questions, she learned to find another doctor.

Most importantly, this woman felt she made her decision to have the surgery from a clear, logical frame of mind. She did not go into it blindly. She acquired a host of people to help her in the recovery, including her daughter. Most parents have a natural desire to not be a burden to their children, but this woman, being afraid of wasting people's time, had an almost neurotic fear. In our work, I encouraged her to see her daughter's help as a rite of passage - a necessary step in the evolution of their relationship. In fact, she eventually became grateful that she had a daughter who was so willing to care for her.

People are fragile beings. We are not rocks here for all eternity. We are born, live, and then die – that is how we are designed. Because all mammals experience life through a lens of emotions, they are all capable of being traumatized and storing this trauma in their bodies or in their mindset. If you have ever seen a traumatized puppy grow into an adult dog, you know that, for all of us mammals, environments and experiences shape perceptions and behavior.

People, however, have more complex brains than dogs. Our minds interpret the world through the lens of the subconscious. We are capable of justifying our perceptions intellectually, of projecting our own experience on others, and of believing the stories we tell ourselves. Our bodies may very well give us clues that our perception of life is inaccurate – a flare up of IBS, fatigue, or depression. Until we can understand the language our body is using to communicate with us, we will continue to ignore its messages. Hypnosis can both help the mind learn to listen to the body's signals and reprogram negative input the brain has on the body.

8

It Helps Motivated People

SUCCESS

Achieve Their Goals

"Always bear in mind that your own resolution to succeed is more important than any other."

—ABRAHAM LINCOLN

Athletes, such as Tiger Woods, and actors, such as Sylvester Stallone, have long used hypnotherapy as a tool to stay focused and achieve their goals. My teacher's teacher, Gil Boyne, did hypnosis on Stallone and that helped him write and then launch the Rocky series.[24] In fact, Stallone continued to use hypnosis throughout the production of the movie to stave off anxiety. After all, it can be as daunting to achieve a goal as to fail. Tiger Woods' father Earl was friends with a Naval psychological agent, who taught Tiger the same techniques of self-hypnosis that were used for special ops in the military. Tiger Woods would go into a "zone" which was really self-induced hypnosis that allowed him to stay calm, focused and unflappable.[25]

What's remarkable is that such individuals recognize that they are the source of their own fear and anxiety. They also know they can be the source of their own success, but that they are somehow blocking themselves from achieving it. They recognize that unnecessary guilt or lack of self-worth can alter split-second timing or create flickers of doubt that resonate in the perceptions of those they're trying to compete with or persuade. One key to success is accepting failure. It's important to accept the fact that there may be many ups and downs on the way to success. One doesn't just wake up in the morning and have everything one wants. Growing into success matters. To quote that old Miley Cyrus song, "It's the Climb." And so, by removing or reversing all fear, be it of succeeding or failing, a state of flow emerges. High pressure activities become a satisfying adventure during which the adventurer enjoys every challenge along the way.

---

[24] https://www.gilboyneonline.com/how-gil-boyne-helped-stallone-become-rocky-balboa/

[25] https://okmagazine.com/p/tiger-woods-hypnotizes-himself-golf-course/

For myself, I use hypnosis to work on any goal, once that goal becomes clear. For example, some time ago, I was asked by the president of my women's club to succeed her as president. I actually had a premonition that she was going to ask me the night before. During her speech to the state chapter of the club, she dropped my name several times... Then she came over to me about an hour later and asked. After that, I got very sick – my digestion went to hell in a handbasket.

Taking on this role, I knew I'd probably be doing a lot of things I would dislike. Yet, I also knew I wanted to do the job and that, of the available people, I probably was the best choice. Then why didn't I celebrate? Well, the answer has multiple parts. First, my husband and I were still new to the state, and I was building my business. I had more than enough to be going on with. How could a 60-something woman with autoimmune disease succeed at two jobs at the same time?

Second, like many of my clients, I had kind of a rough early life where self-esteem is concerned. Though I'd certainly received most physical things I desired growing up, I was continually told by my family that there was no way I would amount to much in life, that my ideas were too different from other people's, that I didn't fit in, that I didn't have qualities other people wanted. For one of my brothers, humiliating me was a daily sport. A small part of me feared success, despite having done the impossible by putting my autoimmune disease into remission and raising two kids.

So, I set to work creating different hypnotic scripts to reverse these clearly false and limiting beliefs. Before I knew it, my digestion improved, and others in the club began to tell me they would like to see me take a leadership role. The universe, as it were, began to support my decision. After a while, I began to be happy about this opportunity. Not only did I do it, but I did it while successfully developing a business from scratch.

It's a remarkable story, really. The keys to success were:

1) acknowledging my fears had no basis in practical fact,
2) reversing the idea that because I had illness I should not overexert myself. This meant changing my psychological relationship to the activities I was engaged in so they wouldn't tire me out, and
3) reversing the idea that bad things might happen to me if I became a public figure, albeit a local one.

In the end, I discovered that I am actually quite suited to this work. I enjoy it. I enjoy initiating activities and ideas. I enjoy changing people's lives for the better. Now that I've reversed these faulty beliefs, I feel more relaxed and at home in my own body. It took a while to register that change. Frankly, I wasn't used to feeling happy in those situations. But, soon, good feelings became status quo, and I just felt satisfied with that work.

I can't imagine enjoying the same kind of success with talk therapy alone. For one, seeing a therapist who may create a codependent relationship is simply at odds with the idea of being an independent leader. How could I ever feel comfortable leading if I had to check my emotions with a therapist beforehand? So, if I was going to lead, I would have to heal myself. Laying out my own limiting beliefs, and knowing how to address them within the system of hypnotherapy, I achieved fairly quick results. After all, the point was to be independent and be comfortable as a leader – easy ideas to instill.

For some reason, I have had many clients who are doctors. This makes sense to me because we have things in common: doctors have to live by a lot of standards and procedures, and of course they want to heal others. So, they feel there's no one to blame but themselves if they can't fulfill the life that they've chosen. It also makes sense because busy doctors need quick results, and they often learned in medical school that self-hypnosis is a great tool for soothing test anxiety. For example, a University of Erlangen-Nurnberg clinical trial on first-year medical students showed those who received hypnosis outperformed those who didn't.[26]

One client, who was a surgeon, needed to pass an oral certification test. He had failed it before, but he didn't just fail it. According to him, he blew it. He had been so nervous that he couldn't speak in complete sentences. He broke out in sweats. He made inappropriate comments. Also, the style of the test disturbed him. Formerly in-person at one time, these tests went online during the pandemic. My client had to endure a life-changing exam given by faces on a screen - not fellow doctors. As you can imagine, a person in this position has more at stake than just the test. Doctors invest years of study and mountains of money. They do residencies that demand long hours in sometimes brutal conditions. They can't afford to make mistakes while on the job because the life of the patient is often at stake. Plus, they have families and children who depend on them. It's a lot of stress.

We worked on his subconscious fears of losing his job. We worked on his relationship with his family, past and present. We discovered a life's purpose of caring for others. We worked on his relationship with the faces on the screen to see them as fellow human beings and doctors. I gave him an anchor (that's a physical means of triggering a positive response in the nervous

[26] https://pubmed.ncbi.nlm.nih.gov/32804002/

system). He could use it if the doctors giving the test said or did something that startled him or shook his confidence. That way he'd stay focused and on track.

The ending of the story is mixed. The client got through the test with ease. He had an appropriate amount of nervousness (in a tough situation, one needs some adrenaline to focus and perform.) He presented himself well. He was cool, confident and personable during the interview. But he didn't pass the test. Why? I can't say – perhaps some flaw in his education or something political going on with the judges. Yet, he told me that the work we did together changed his life. He intends to incorporate hypnosis in his work with his future patients. He also intends to take the test again.

Whether this man takes the test or not is immaterial. What matters is that he is fulfilling his life's purpose as a caring individual. Perhaps some higher power is leading him to a better place. Who knows? I have no judgment on the outcome. All I know is that I fulfilled my end of it: he dropped his fear of taking the test and answered all the questions professionally and to the best of his ability. He thanked me profusely because, win or lose, he had mastered his emotions and done his best.

So, you can see that every individual measures success differently. Success is not always winning a game, passing a test, or making a lot of money. Success is not fulfilling a life that other people want for you. Success is a feeling of forward motion and accomplishment as well as a feeling of pride and fulfillment.

Many people come to hypnotherapy thinking they want to succeed in a certain task, sport, or career, and then several sessions into the process, we discover that that is not the goal at all. They want to feel satisfied. They want to feel at peace. They want a sense of forward motion. They want their real talents to manifest. They want to relieve some long-standing doubt. In fact, it's hard to list the many things that clients want when pursuing success because every want is so individual to each client.

One thing is clear, however. If clients cannot picture success and feel it viscerally, success will remain out of reach. If they can, success, however it is defined, appears easily, naturally, and fairly quickly, changing their lives for the good forever.

9

It Reveals Hidden Resources

"All the resources we need are in the mind."

—THEODORE ROOSEVELT

Julia Child and Colonel Sanders are two people who found success later in life. They lived a good part of their lives, at least until middle age, using their skills in a certain way, and then suddenly appear to go in a different direction. Colonel Sanders in particular was old even by today's standards when he started Kentucky Fried Chicken. To an outsider, it might seem as if he suddenly discovered a new talent or inner resource. But in fact, that resource was there all along. If that resource had been buried, discovering it could feel like finally living the life you were meant to live.

As a famous chef, Julia Child's first foray into cooking was when she created shark repellent for the OSS during World War II. It wasn't until she was nearly 40 and living in Paris that she experienced a kind of spiritual awakening when she tasted French haute cuisine. What made Child important, however, was combining this passion for cooking with her innate ability to network and entertain. Moreover, she was open-minded about television when television was new.[27]

Harlan Sanders, born in 1890, came up with the idea of selling his "secret recipe" fried chicken from a roadside restaurant during the Great Depression. He was in his 40s. But his real genius wasn't cooking. He also came up with the idea of franchising, and after his original restaurant closed, he set to franchising Kentucky Fried Chicken all over the US. It wasn't until Sanders was 73 that this now national business became too much for him.[28]

---

[27] https://juliachildfoundation.org
[28] https://uh.edu/hilton-college/About/Hospitality-Industry-Hall-of-Honor/Inductees/Colonel-Harland-Sanders%20/

Neither Child nor Sanders limited their lives with limiting beliefs. Of course, they may have been limited by belief systems of the times in which they lived. For example, Julia Child, who had no children of her own, had time to be a celebrity chef, and she appealed to women who were home raising families in the 50s and 60s. Harlan Sanders may not have invented franchising, but he took advantage of the postwar need for returning soldiers to establish businesses quickly. Child and Sanders didn't hold limiting beliefs about their careers, yet they also embraced reality.

Drawing on the personal anecdote from the previous chapter, I was raised with a lot of limiting beliefs about my own potential. For example, in a dinnertime discussion when I was about 12, I was asked how much money I thought I could make once I became an adult. My answer was that I would make $100,000 a year. And I came up with this amount because it was a period of inflation, and I projected what money would be worth in 20 years. Plus, I had some idea of what my father made, how much our house was worth, and an idea of what was an appropriate ratio between salary and homeownership.

The response was guffaws from everyone at the table. What was interesting was that they didn't think my number was unreasonable for a talented successful male in the future. But it was unreasonable for me as a female to even think about it. I can only say that, looking back on my life, I was living with good people who lacked empathy. None of them were evil in any obvious sense. But now that I know a little bit about Psychology, I know the way I acquired so many limiting beliefs was growing up around people who not only had limiting ideas about women, they just couldn't see through another's eyes.

And yet, something inside me always drew me to situations where the leadership was lacking, and I'd think "I can do this better." Because I carried so many false beliefs around leadership, I would think that I wasn't meant to lead, and doing so felt like I was dragging a ton of bricks. It probably took many years for me to recognize leadership as my natural state. One reason I enjoy doing hypnotherapy is that I can lead leaders. Many of my clients are doctors, as I've said. I know that I help them be better at their work, and that my work trickles down to the lives of many other people – people I don't even know. I am here to make an impact, and thanks to hypnotherapy, I now celebrate this fact rather than run from it.

When people are in a relaxed state - lightly focused on something like doing the laundry, perhaps - the brain's "default mode network" kicks in.[29] We start making connections, reviewing our lives, telling ourselves little stories about ourselves or others. Without even knowing it, we make decisions about these things, for better or worse. In hypnosis, we stand back and observe the mind's activities. We recognize faulty beliefs and the source of negative programming. More importantly, in doing so, we can change these beliefs. We can change them to what we know is true and healthy for us. No, I can't make myself taller or some other unreasonable goal. But if it's true that I'm good at art, for example, and I suppress it, my body will suffer from the act of suppression. According to Bruce Lipton, every cell in my body will know I'm doing it.[30]

---

[29] https://neuroscientificallychallenged.com/posts/know-your-brain-default-mode-network
[30] Lipton, Bruce Ph.D. The Biology of Belief. 10th ed., Hay House, 2015.

Living authentically often comes with a price. I currently have a client who isn't sure if her husband is cheating on her. As is sometimes the case, she came in for other reasons, but that's the real problem. Rather, seeing herself as the type of person who would choose a man who would cheat on her (whether he's actually doing it or not) is her problem. Her whole body, it seems, is rebelling against the situation as she's experiencing multiple digestive problems and has pain in her neck. What are her options? It isn't as simple as leave and find a new guy because whatever attracted her to this situation is still there.

This young woman needs to discover what causes her to be drawn to such men, change her relationship to it, and then discover inner resources that will help her either take action or let it go. If she is making things up about her partner, she needs to discover why – what moment in her past, maybe even in her ancestral past, justifies this kind of paranoia? Or maybe she's actually in love with a man who cheats on her. In which case, she's got to accept her fate or leave. One thing is for sure, she can't change him. He is who he is. And she is who she is. She can't even begin to have compassion for him until she has compassion for herself.

What's amazing about hypnotherapy is that the therapist never need tell her what to do. Ultimately, her subconscious will reveal her true nature, and she will decide.

In talk therapy, there is always the danger that the client will simply exchange the bad relationship with the husband (or whomever) for a relationship with the therapist. They end up seeing the therapist for years without experiencing real personal freedom. Friends have shared with me – and, sadly, I know from having my own marital difficulties – that not all marriage counselors want to see marriages thrive. They are human beings with their own experiences and biases.

Though the job of counselors and therapists is to hold up a neutral mirror to the relationship, some would side with the wife, others the husband. I remember saying to one therapist that I was determined to change a certain aspect of my own behavior, and his response was a chuckle, saying that all of his female clients end up in divorce. He had completely misheard me. He thought the only way of achieving my goal was to get rid of the father of my children to whom I'd been married for half my life. The therapist, being divorced himself, was likely projecting his situation onto mine. So instead, I used hypnosis to change my belief system. As I changed, the relationship changed, slowly but surely, until my husband and I found each other again.

In hypnotherapy, clients really heal themselves. There's no judgment. It's whatever works – for that person. It's all really a matter of the client rediscovering resources, and then focusing on expanding those resources instead of focusing on the limiting beliefs.

Some clients have what I call a very difficult karma. I don't mean karma in the sense of what goes around comes around – that if I'm nice to others, others will be nice to me. I mean it as a synonym for tendency. We all have a tendency for certain things to happen because of the time we live in, because of the city or surroundings we live in, because of the family we are born into, and because of the physical body that we are born with. For example, at the time of this writing, the nation is recovering from the COVID-19 pandemic and inflation is very much on the rise. All of that is happening around me; I didn't cause it. Yet, the times influence my emotions and my thinking. They trigger subconscious beliefs, and how I respond to them matters.

Children born during the pandemic would naturally have a very different experience of early life than those born before or after it. Add in the uniqueness of each family situation - whether the extended family is big or small or if mom and dad get along or not, and that contributes further karma. And lastly, what type of body does this baby have? Strong or weak? Vivacious or calm? How a child feels in its body influences how it reacts to situations. Not every child likes roller coasters, for example. Not every child is good at sports. So, every second of our lives makes us unique. And, some people, as I said, have a very, very difficult karma.

The parents of one of my clients married and divorced several times over the course of her childhood. Another client had a father who sexually abused her. One man had an alcoholic father who beat him. And all of these very personal, very painful events are surrounded by a culture that collectively influences the individuals within it. For the man, his father's behavior at the time and in the place that it happened was fairly commonplace. So, it was easier for him to be forgiving about his dad's behavior than, say, the woman whose father abused her. After working with so many people, one begins to see that life is a web of intentions, behaviors, and outcomes. There is beauty to the truth in even some of the most horrific situations.

The reason I call it beautiful is that beneath the horror and pain often lie phenomenal hidden resources. The client with the divorced parents seemed to be able to sense from the womb what she called "the coming storm." She became sensitive to energetic vibrations – the emotions that others give off even before they process those emotions themselves. Her empathy made her a terrific mother and inspired her to study different types of energy healing work. The man who was beaten by his father took on a life of selfless service. The woman who was abused by her father ultimately became an inspiring teacher.

In hypnosis, these strengths appear and can even be a surprise to the client. One woman discovered that her inner strength was graciousness. She was not particularly a gracious person, not to me anyway. And from the stories she told me about her interactions with her family, I believe her self-perception was that she was awkward and a little selfish. Yet, discovering graciousness as a hidden resource changed her life. It gave her the ability to ask questions, particularly of doctors, rather than frame herself as a victim. It's empowering to take on behavior that works.

One's inner resources help one face all the difficult karma. The resources also help one create healthy boundaries, to know one's limitations as well as one's area of expertise. By enhancing her graciousness, this client learned to say "no." She also began to see that she could help others help her by complimenting them. She learned that inner strength comes from following through with one's intentions, and that doing it with kindness and empathy made success a lot easier. She didn't have to be tough with people. She could be gracious and determined at the same time.

Another client continually told me that she "overreacted" to life events. First, it seemed clear that someone else was telling her this. She would simply berate herself if she had an emotional reaction to people or situations. Granted, she did have a temper. But that doesn't mean she was overreacting. Labeling her responses as overreacting made her distrust her own intuition.

Ultimately, we discovered that she was a very sensitive and emotional person; after all, she was an artist.

We learned that it wasn't so much that she overreacted but that she didn't react quickly enough. She didn't respect her own emotions, which were key to her character. She would suppress them until they'd burst out. The key to her transformation was acknowledging her exceptional intuition and giving herself space to act upon it. When one has a unique voice, as she had, it's easy to suppress that voice in favor of getting along with first one's family and then one's friends and co-workers. Seeing her emotions as a gift allowed her to let them flow through her and inform her so that she could draw boundaries and take action more quickly and effectively.

Famed American psychologist and hypnotherapy pioneer Milton Erikson was noted for his compassionate and surprisingly simple means of working with clients. He created "teaching tales" or anecdotes about his own family life or cases of previous patients that carried with them meaning for the patient's problem. They often included a shock or surprise, giving the patient an "aha" moment that got them to think. Not only would they glean the message, but they would also apply it to their life as a resource without being told to do so.

When a hospital was building a new wing, Erickson got a man who claimed to be 'Jesus' to help out with the carpentry, knowing that the man could not deny that Jesus was famously a carpenter before coming out as the Messiah. This unusual remedy got the man engaged with reality and other people again. More importantly, it preserved his dignity and played to his strengths.

The man made his own choices and, though Erickson was the catalyst, he drew on his inner resources to heal.[31]

Karma is real and often inevitable. As my mother used to say, "Into each one's life a little rain must fall." Yet, beneath every negative reaction or behavior is a hidden resource, a gift, that can help mitigate life's challenges and help you grow from them. Cultivating this gift can improve life fairly rapidly, and it can help put negative reactions and behaviors into perspective. They seem transitory. They become just a sign that you're a little out of sorts. The real YOU knows that developing those hidden resources is one of the greatest gifts in life.

---

[31] Rosen, S. (2010). My Voice Will Go with You: The Teaching Tales of Milton H. Erickson. W. W. Norton & Company.

10

It Could Save Your Life

"There are only two days in the year that nothing can be done. one is called yesterday and the other is called tomorrow... so today is the right day to love, believe, do and mostly live."

—DALAI LAMA

Stories of people whose positive mindset saved their lives or got them through harrowing situations abound. The Dalai Lama, for example, had to flee his own country and then wound up as an internationally renowned public figure doing more for Buddhism than any monk who has ever lived. Desmond Tutu, a South African Anglican priest and important opponent of apartheid, became a priest at the age of 39, left South Africa to study theology in Great Britain, then returned to South Africa to make change. The mindset he acquired studying theology gave him the courage to become a human rights activist on a scale that ultimately won him the Nobel Peace Prize. The Reverend Martin Luther King, Jr., also drew upon his faith to inspire him to lead the civil rights movement and, as a byproduct, become one of the most transformative figures in the history of the United States. These examples cite religious leaders, but it is not necessary to be religious to change your mindset. It requires dedication and practice such as meditation, prayer, or hypnosis – all of which awakens the superconscious: our connection to universal intelligence. The superconscious is key to healing, to knowing one is in the right place at the right time, and to building inner courage so strong that facing potential death becomes bearable.

When I was studying at the Hypnotherapy Academy of America, our teacher Tim Simmerman-Sierra showed a video of himself getting fillings replaced without the use of anesthetic. His only source of pain relief was his hypnotic trance. He then showed another video of his wife doing it, too. So that's proof that at least two people on the planet can have teeth drilled without drugs. I am a hypnotherapist, and I know how to do what they did, but I don't intend to follow in their footsteps.

Yet, in a way I have. And, sooner than I expected.

I have come close to death three times. In the first, I wasn't really in danger. I had a flu that attacked the vagus nerve, and without warning, my blood pressure dropped and I collapsed. Both my husband and I thought I was having a stroke. There was no time to think or say good-bye. When I came out of it, I was surrounded by the three handsomest paramedics in San Francisco. Lucky me. But that was the first time I experienced the powerful state of being totally present. Something about approaching death clears our minds of all but what matters most. And, I wasn't afraid.

The second time was in 2013 when a tourist ran a red light near San Francisco's Union Square and struck my car on the driver's side. I remember looking down and seeing, in slow motion, the door pressing towards me. I actually thought, "Maybe I should get out of the way." A second later, I was staring up at the traffic light with the engine smoking. I was totally in shock and, with the driver's door crushed, people had to help me out of the car. Since I didn't black out, the ER doctors told me I was largely fine. But in fact, I had a severe concussion, whiplash, and a great strain to my back. It took me about eight months to recover. For the first several months, my left brain was practically useless – if I even thought about math, I got a migraine. I entertained myself by doing art. With my left brain out of commission, my ability to paint blossomed. In a matter of months, I achieved a near professional level, which stays with me to this day.

The story of my sudden growth as an artist could be a book in itself. Yet, with respect to hypnosis and the study of the mind, other things were happening to me. As a suddenly right-brained individual, my personality also changed for a while, and this showed me how much the brain/mind influences thought, behavior, and perception. In my healing journey, some scientists at the lab where my husband worked gave me an EEG device that measured brainwaves. I could see an image of my brain on a screen and play with how to heal the damaged side. I found breathing exercise and meditation/prayer were key to recovery. In other words, I used alpha and theta brainwaves to slowly heal my brain.

When the third brush with death occurred, I was a certified hypnotherapist. A freak course of events led me to vomit and tear my esophagus. I was brought by ambulance, in the snow, and wearing nothing but a t-shirt and panties to a hospital in Santa Fe that had neither the equipment nor the surgical staff to save me. So, after a six-hour search of surrounding hospitals, they flew me to a hospital in Colorado Springs, where a surgeon saved my life. It took two months for me to walk properly and six months to regain the 20 pounds I lost after the surgery. The stress of the whole affair had slowed my stomach's ability to function. I was diagnosed with gastroparesis and a GI doctor predicted more surgeries. Additionally, my insurance company and the hospital didn't communicate well with each other. We were threatened with astronomical bills. My husband and I were terrified the costs would bankrupt us.

Of course, hypnotherapy played a crucial part in my survival and recovery. During the long wait for a hospital, I had been given pain medicine, and that relaxed the spasm in my back, but did absolutely nothing for my septic stomach. So, whenever anyone wasn't asking me my birthday or poking me with a needle, I did self-hypnosis. In fact, I did the protocol that my teacher did when he had his teeth worked on. I did my best to numb my body by giving it the experience of being on a beach in Hawaii, a place I've never been to.

It was challenging to achieve a trance state, because my lungs were rapidly shrinking away from the spreading stomach acid. If I had to speak, I could only say one word at a time. Plus, the vagus nerve, which basically constitutes the parasympathetic nervous system, was not just a little bit damaged – it was very damaged, with my lungs, my esophagus, my stomach and all the strain to my heart and other internal organs. But I have five senses and I utilized my imagination to create images and sensations that overrode the extreme pain. I felt the wind caressing my body as it flowed off the beach. I felt the warming, calming sunshine. I heard the gentle crashing of the waves. I saw myself there in a bathing suit and a sunhat. I smelled the tanning oil and the salty air. I did this for the better part of 12 hours.

When I met the surgeon in Colorado, he didn't believe the diagnosis because I was so calm and upbeat. He actually made me go through the diagnostic tests again before telling me there was a possibility I could die on the operating table. I told him I already knew that, that I wouldn't be angry if I died. I told him we should think and say only positive thoughts and just see what happens.

While awaiting surgery, I texted a colleague - just before my phone died - and asked for a recording to be sent to my husband. He made sure I had it in recovery, and I continued to listen to it during my hospital stay. Not only did I recover in record time, I recovered faster and better than anyone anticipated. After I was strong enough, I created recordings that would reverse some of those negative prognoses. I kept myself, as much as possible, in the present moment and from taking those dark nocebos too seriously.

During this time, not only did I use self-hypnosis for my physical recovery, but I used it to improve our precarious finances. On the advice of one friend and with the help of another, I agreed to produce a GoFundMe to raise money for the alternative treatments that would be key to my recovery. I had never thought of myself as being able to raise money, especially in such a public manner. I was already dealing with negative self-talk and feelings of low self-esteem just from being in this situation. So, in short, I used hypnotherapy sessions and recordings to fuel my confidence. I went from feeling unworthy of help, and not wanting to appear a loser or a burden, to graciously allowing a flood of support from friends across the country and from all seasons of my life. The results paid for my physical healing and permanently changed my self-perception. I now think of raising money as one of my skills.

Without hypnotherapy, none of that could have been possible. While I admit to having experienced the occasional dark day or black mood during that time, my predominant post-hypnosis mindset was that I would recover and that I would continue my career as a hypnotherapist in Santa Fe. Although I have surgical scars, my digestion has returned to where it was prior to the incident. In fact, I now eat plenty of fiber and healthy oils, both of which are forbidden on a gastroparesis diet. My energy has returned in full, and I have little to no residual pain.

How did hypnosis save my life exactly? First, I used it to distract my mind and body from excruciating pain and the thought of inevitable death. Yes, I did experience pain, but it was manageable. By diverting the pain, I'm convinced that I also prevented lifelong chronic pain. I simply didn't allow pain to make inroads in my brain's real estate. Second, by staying positive and calm, I didn't add more stress to my body; in fact, I probably reversed a great deal of it.

Moreover, the nurses, the staff, the paramedics - all around me - were happy to help me. I only expected reasonable things from them. I didn't, for example, expect them magically to make the pain go away. I didn't expect the surgeon to save my life. I lightened the load for him and the staff by showing them I had genuine confidence in them. Third, I used hypnosis in my recovery. My positive attitude made everyone who walked in the door of my hospital room smile.

One time, I remember having to do my mandatory stroll around the ward. The first day or two, I literally needed three people because I had so much stuff hooked up to me. But soon I only needed two, and then one. Yet, sometimes I would have three helpers. I could see they were all inspired by how well I was doing. Inspiring them inspired me. My attitude came as a result of hypnosis because my recovery recordings included the suggestion that I had diligent, cheerful staff taking care of me.

Once I was out of the hospital, and staying in an Airbnb in Colorado Springs, I used hypnosis to motivate me to keep walking. Walking was excruciating because the surgeon had gone in through my left side ribs to suck out all the stomach acid and the accumulating mess. That totally threw off the alignment of my spine and gave me permanent floating ribs. Because I knew it was essential to keep walking, I motivated myself to do so. Additionally, I used hypnosis to reverse programming that would inhibit my recovery. Doctors and nurses, and even the chiropractor I saw to help realign my back, all had negative things to say that I could've taken to heart. "You might not survive the surgery." "You're never going to eat normally again." "You'll never gain the weight back." "Don't expect yourself to exercise in the same way you did before." "Your back is deformed." If I had bought into any of it, I might've died or remained stuck in a vicious circle of negativity. Here, talk therapy didn't apply. There was really nothing that a talk therapist could do for me from the time I threw up until I returned to Santa Fe. Only hypnosis could've helped.

Thanks to hypnosis, I have the opinion that the greatest thing one can do in life is live well to the best of one's ability and, at the end, let go graciously. I had a client who very much wanted a past life session in order to revisit his death in a Spitfire during World War II. I don't typically do past life sessions because so many people want them out of vanity. They want to think of themselves all dressed up and perhaps suffering during some former life so they can blame everything in the current life on that experience. I would normally be very hesitant about giving a past life session to a person who "knew for a fact" that they had a very particular death or life before this one. Yet, I did do a past life session on this client, and the results explained everything about his attitude towards life in this life.

Before I go any further, I want to say I have an exceptionally open mind about past lives. My son, when he was between 3 ½ and five, talked very clearly of past lives – so clearly that anyone who was around at the time remarked on it. He first expressed this while we were having an outing at the Queen Mary steamship museum. I held him up to look at a display of photographs of tall ships. He began labeling the parts, something I'm sure they don't teach in preschool. There were other incidents, too, but without going into it too deeply, I can say that I thought of other ways that seeming "past life" information could get into the head of a three-year-old. I'm not attached to past lives as a reality. But if I think exploring a past life is going to help a client, I will provide it.

In the case of this client, revisiting his death in the Spitfire gave him insight into his behavior towards his wife. He was constantly afraid of losing her. He was afraid that he would go to work and never come back, every single day. And it wasn't his death he was afraid of; it was letting her down, the way he had let his 1940s fiancé down when he never came back. In his session, he revealed an arrogant former self, just as young soldiers may very well be, to maintain his courage. He wasn't afraid to die, but he was sure he was coming back. Interestingly, when I tried to reverse the negative belief systems his subconscious had acquired, whether through past life or something else, he strongly resisted the change. He was afraid that, if he dropped that fear, he might lose his wife again in this lifetime. Coming out of the trance, I'm happy to say that he saw the connections between the present and former ideas of himself. He knew he must change - though he preferred to do it more slowly with his wife at his side.

Hypnosis did not save his life so much as change his relationship to death. In that sense, it gave him a richer, fuller, and more satisfying life. He saw that his wife and children had to live their own lives and that doing so involved taking a certain degree of risk. None of us live forever, so it's important to live well, to live by one's values, to be happy and healthy, and then say goodbye with grace and ease when the time comes.

My teachers offered example after example of clients who saw their cancer go into remission or their back pain vanish, as well as clients who conquered ADHD or phobias, or clients who built new lives after incest, etc. I'm reluctant to make those kinds of extreme promises - potential lawsuits aside - because I believe those problems are secondary to being your own person and knowing how to function as your own person in a complicated world. That's what I mean by living well. It's not about being rich, successful, or good looking; it's about being happy in your own skin, knowing what your values are and living them, letting go of bitterness and resentment, being here now rather than being trapped in a fantasy of how things should be. To fully accept the human condition means to accept that death is inevitable, and that it's not necessarily a bad thing. It's what makes life so valuable after all.

AFTERWORD

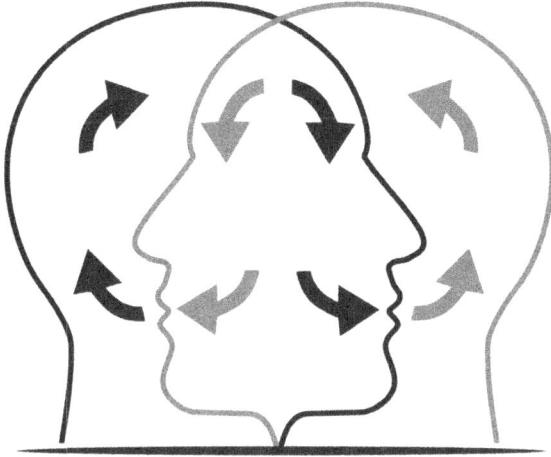

When I was a kid, I never would've thought of becoming a hypnotherapist. The idea would've just seemed too far-fetched. Yet, today, this life and this mode of helping others make complete sense. In fact, my practice as a hypnotherapist, supported by my own personal self-hypnosis, has made me happier than I've been in my life.

Hypnotherapy is easy, fast-working, powerful, and positive. The work, since it appeals to the whole brain as well as the mind, is both creative and analytical. It can be applied prescriptively, utilized to solve specific problems, or it can be used artistically, to create a new functional personality from a dysfunctional or destructive one. It's collaborative, in that the therapist and client work together. It's liberating. Since all the work happens within clients' minds, clients really heal themselves. It's practical, effective, quick, and relatively affordable compared to other mind healing modalities.

Probably the most amazing thing about hypnotherapy is how naturally clients experience change. Recently, a client felt reluctant to let go of sessions. She didn't feel entirely "cooked" even though she had achieved her goal. I asked her to think of what was missing, what she still needed to feel whole as a person. She came up with it, and in our last session together, we nailed it. At the end, she smiled a most blissful smile and said, "I'm done now. I'll call you if I need you." We both knew she had truly transformed, and that she had completed her transformation. Moreover, she has tools, in the form of recordings and techniques that she can use to keep herself on track. Trance is a natural state of mind that clients can learn to harness for their own betterment.

Clients experience true miracles. They reduce stress and chronic pain. Their view of life changes, and they make stunning realizations: human beings really can heal themselves; physical ailments are sometimes in our minds; and it's not only okay to relax, it's essential for our well-being. They conquer fears and achieve personal and career goals. They learn they have hidden strengths and resources that they can access in their darkest times. Their relationships improve because their relationship with themselves improves. They rediscover faith in themselves and possibly faith in a higher power. And this comes in handy if life has dealt them particularly difficult challenges. A client with terminal cancer finds peace and acceptance, and with that, sometimes physical healing. Courage doesn't feel like courage; it feels like a natural approach to overcoming any obstacle. And, yes, you might even use it to help save your life.

About the Author

Anne Nygren Doherty is a medical support and clinical hypnotherapist based in New Mexico and working around the US and Canada. She is also a Reiki practitioner, a Sat Nam Rasayan practitioner, and a long-time Kundalini yoga instructor.

Mother of two adult children and married to a former Silicon Valley researcher, she came to hypnotherapy in response to health issues and two near-fatal accidents. However, her ability to write, create, and appreciate the power of the subconscious mind was honed during her professional theater career, which exposed her to many alternative modes of healing, such as the Alexander Technique and the Feldenkrais Method. She owned The Alcove Theater in San Francisco and was the artistic director of the Musical Theater of San Francisco.

You can learn more about hypnotherapy and read her blog at www.RestoreHypnotherapy.com.

References

Atwater, PMH. (2013) *Future Memory*. Hampton Roads.

Dispenza, Joe. (2017). *Becoming Supernatural.* HAY HOUSE UK LTD.

Dispenza, Joe. (2018). *You Are the Placebo: Making Your Mind Matter.* Hay House, Inc.

Doidge, N., M.D. (2015). *The Brain's Way of Healing.* Viking, an Imprint of Penguin Group.

Gabor Maté. (2019). *When the Body Says No: The Cost of Hidden Stress.* Vermilion.

Lipton, Bruce Ph.D. (2015). *The Biology of Belief (10th ed).* Hay House.

Rosen, S. (2010). *My Voice Will Go with You: The Teaching Tales of Milton H. Erickson.* W. W. Norton & Company.

Anbar, R. D. *Spirituality and Hypnosis*. https://www.psychologytoday.com/us/blog/understanding-hypnosis/202112/spirituality-and-hypnosis

Deaconess, B. E. *Program in Placebo Studies & Therapeutic Encounter (PiPS)*. http://programinplacebostudies.org/

Dispenza, J. *Evidence is the Loudest Voice.* https://drjoedispenza.com/pages/scientific-research

Dispenza, J. *Research News & Updates.* https://drjoedispenza.com/blogs/research

Goleman, D. *Relaxing: Surprising Benefits Detected.* https://www.nytimes.com/1986/05/13/science/relaxation-surprising-benefits-detected.html

Hammer, C.M., Scholz, M., Bischofsberger, L., Paulsen, F., Burger, P. *Feasibility of Clinical Hypnosis for Test Anxiety in First-Year Medical Students.* https://pubmed.ncbi.nlm.nih.gov/32804002/

Heid,M. *Is Hypnosis Real? Here's What Science Says.* https://time.com/5380312/is-hypnosis-real-science/

Shauna L. Shapiro, Gary E. Schwartz & Ginny Bonner. *Effects of Mindfulness-Based Stress Reduction on Medical and Premedical Students.* https://link.springer.com/article/10.1023/A:1018700829825

G A van Montfrans, J M Karemaker, W Wieling, A J Dunning. *Relaxation therapy and continuous ambulatory blood pressure in mild hypertension: a controlled study.* https://www.bmj.com/content/300/6736/1368

Kirsch, I. *Clinical hypnosis as a nondeceptive placebo: Empirically derived techniques.* https://psycnet.apa.org/record/1995-14577-001

Lee, M. *Calming Your Nerves and Your Heart Through Meditation.* https://sitn.hms.harvard.edu/flash/2009/issue61/

What is the function of the various brainwaves? https://www.scientificamerican.com/article/what-is-the-function-of-t-1997-12-22/

https://www.ncbi.nlm.nih.gov/pmc/articles/PMC4575591/

https://www.heartmath.org

How Gil Boyne helped Stallone become Rocky Balboa. https://www.gilboyneonline.com/how-gil-boyne-helped-stallone-become-rocky-balboa/

Colonel Harland Sanders: Founder of Kentucky Fried Chicken. https://uh.edu/hilton-college/About/Hospitality-Industry-Hall-of-Honor/Inductees/Colonel-Harland-Sanders%20/

Tiger Woods Hypnotizes Himself On Golf Course Using Same Technique As Special Op Forces. https://okmagazine.com/p/tiger-woods-hypnotizes-himself-golf-course/

Hypnosis helps healing: Surgical wounds mend faster. https://news.harvard.edu/gazette/story/2003/05/hypnosis-helps-healing-2/

Hypnosis helps healing: Surgical wounds mend faster. https://news.harvard.edu/gazette/story/2003/05/hypnosis-helps-healing-2/

Know Your Brain: Default Mode Network. https://neuroscientificallychallenged.com/posts/know-your-brain-default-mode-network

The Julia Child Foundation for Gastronomy and the Culinary Arts. https://juliachildfoundation.org

https://anxietycontrolcenter.com/can-anyone-go-into-a-trance-6/

Made in the USA
Coppell, TX
17 January 2024

27647285R10075